Painting
Blooms &
Blossoms

Painting Blooms & Blossoms

JUDY DIEPHOUSE & LYNNE DEPTULA

NORTH LIGHT BOOKS

CINCINNATI, OHIO

www.nlbooks.com

DEDICATION

As we enter a new century, we can't help but remember all of the decorative artists in our past that have inspired and shaped our personal painting style. We dedicate this book to the decorative artists of the future, may we inspire them to paint distinctively and develop their own appreciation of this beautiful art form.

ACKNOWLEDGEMENT

We would like to thank Greg Albert for selecting us to author this book of flowers and fruits. We would also like to gratefully thank our publishing team Kathy Kipp, Heather Dakota, Christine Polomsky and Jane Friedman for making our photoshoot and total publishing experience with North Light Books a true pleasure!

We would also like to lovingly thank our husbands, Frank Deptula and Dave Diephouse for their encouragement and love which enables us to pursue such a delightful career.

Other fine North Light Books are available from your local bookstore, art supply store or direct from the publisher.

04 03 02 01 00   5 4 3 2

Library of Congress Cataloging-in-Publication Data

Diephouse, Judy.
    Painting blooms & blossoms / Judy Diephouse, Lynne Deptula—1st ed.
        p.   cm.
    Includes Index.
    ISBN 0-89134-972-3 (alk. paper).— ISBN 0-89134-989-8 (pbk. : alk. paper)
    1. Flowers in Art. 2. Painting—Technique—Amateur's manuals.
    I. Deptula, Lynne II. Title. III. Title: Painting blooms and blossoms.
ND1400.D54 2000
745.7'23—dc21   99-16726
                                                        CIP

Editor: Kathy Kipp, Heather Dakota
Interior Designer: Brian Roeth
Cover Designer: Kathy DeZarn
Photography: Christine Polomsky
Production Coordinator: John Peavler

ABOUT THE AUTHORS

The friends we meet through painting!! Lynne and Judy first met when Lynne attended a local SDP meeting and Judy was the teacher. Many lessons later they formed the business partnership of Distinctive Brushstrokes, painting mainly for regional art shows and teaching at various regional and national conventions. Eventually, their business evolved into designing pattern packets, writing decorative painting books and travel teaching. Today Distinctive Brushstrokes has published 11 book and over 90 pattern packets! Look for them on the teaching roster of your favorite decorative painting convention. Both ladies live in Grand Rapids with their husbands and families, sharing their love for this wonderful art form.

Judy Diephouse
1674 Hall St. SE
Grand Rapids, MI 49506
Tel: 616-241-2937
Fax: 616-241-4766
E-mail: DistinctJ@aol.com

Lynne Deptula
7245 Cascade Woods Dr. SE
Grand Rapids, MI 49546
Tel: 616-940-1899
Fax: 616-940-6002
E-mail: Dbrush1@aol.com

TABLE OF CONTENTS

INTRODUCTION

The friends we meet through painting are some of the best! We first met at a local Society of Decorative Painters chapter meeting. Many lessons later we formed the business partnership of Distinctive Brushstrokes.

As former school teachers who made a decision to stay home with their children, we found ourselves concentrating on painting for several large art and craft shows in the Midwest. Besides doing art shows each year, we taught at local seminars, the Heart of Ohio Tole Convention and the SDP National Convention. During those years of painting every day, often ten to twelve hours a day, we developed the style and techniques that you'll find in this book.

After many requests for class projects, we decided to try making pattern packets. Over the summer, we designed and published thirty pattern packet designs. We were surprised at the overwhelming response for our designs. After five years, we have published eleven books and more than one hundred pattern packets.

Our goal has always been to provide our students with clear instructions, complete information and achievable results. We take time each year to research the current and developing color and theme trends. With this knowledge, we keep our color palette fresh and current.

We hope you enjoy painting these designs as much as we enjoyed designing them. We want to help you grow as a decorative painter, and we want to share our love of this art form. For more information about decorative painting and the Society of Decorative Painters, please write the Society of Decorative Painters, 393 N. McLean Blvd., Wichita, KS 67203-5968 or call (316) 269-9300.

Chapter One

Materials and Supplies

Paints

We use Delta Ceramcoat, DecoArt Americana and occasionally a specific color in Accent acrylic paint. These are nontoxic, water-based acrylic paints sold in bottles. Shake the bottles well before using to make sure the binder is mixed with the pigments. These paints can be thinned with water for a more transparent look or an ink-like consistency for strokework. Many different products on the market can be mixed with these paints to extend the drying time, or for easier flow. We don't use these products as we prefer using water, but feel free to experiment.

Brushes

All of the brushes used in this book are from Scharff Brushes, Inc., P.O. Box 746, Fayetteville, GA 30214, 1-888-SCHARFF

The series used include:

- #140—flat shader
- #455—liners
- #405—rounds
- #165—comb (rakes)
- #760—deerfoot stippler
- #480—script liner
- #550—wash
- #670—mop

Generally, acrylic brushes are made of synthetic fibers, such as Golden Taklon, because they hold up better when using acrylic paint. Natural hair brushes seem to swell when using water. The condition of your brushes determines the quality of your painting. It is very difficult for anyone to achieve nice strokework with a brush that has swelled or has loose hairs sticking out of it. Several good brands of brushes are on the market, but like many other things, you get what you pay for. To clean the brushes, we recommend DecoArt Americana's Brush Cleaner.

Additional Supplies

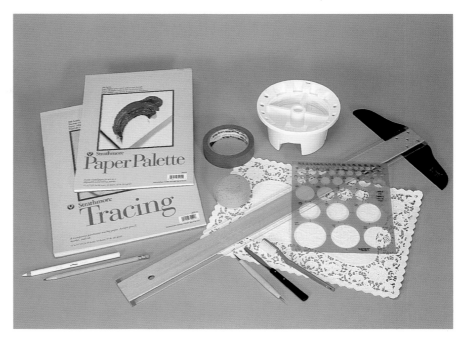

1. Water Basin

Many brands of water basins are available, but a good basin will have ridges across one section of the bottom to push and pull your brush across to loosen and remove the paint from your brush. Grooves should be on one side to hold the brushes in water, preventing the paint from drying in the brush. A high divider in the basin helps keep a supply of clean water.

2. Stylus

A good stylus is helpful for applying the pattern to the project and for any fine dots and details you add to the painting. Often a stylus comes with two ends; one end is finer than the other.

3. Palette Knife

A palette knife comes in handy when you are asked to make a color mixture.

4. T-square

A T-square will help make your design or lines straight on the painting surface. It is available at most office supply stores.

5. Circle Template

A circle template is useful for making perfect circles.

6. Sponge

A small round sponge is used to apply clouds and foliage to some of the projects.

7. Pencils

Always have a supply of sharpened no. 2 graphite and chalk pencils in your paint box. When tracing a pattern, one small area may be omitted. Instead of trying to replace the pattern exactly, you can freehand the extra line.

8. Paper Doily

We recommend the rectangular place mat doily which gives you a long section to place around the box to create the detail.

9. Transparent Tape

We recommend using quality transparent tape. Place the tape where you need it, and seal the edge with your finger to prevent paint from bleeding underneath the tape.

10. Toothbrush

An old toothbrush is the best tool for splattering or fly-specking. Add a little water to your paint, tap the front end of the brush into it. You may want to touch the brush on a paper towel to remove excess paint. With the bristles of the toothbrush pointing up, run your nail across the bristles to make the paint splatter. You may want to practice this on paper before you try it on a project. The more water you add to the paint, the larger the splatter dots.

11. Palette

We use disposable waxed palettes. We do not use a wet palette because we often blend colors on the brush before painting. If the palette is wet, it is difficult to achieve a nice blend.

12. Tracing Paper

Tracing paper comes in a variety of sizes readily available at art and office supply stores. After you trace the design, place it on the prepared surface. You can tape one edge to keep the pattern steady. Slide a piece of graphite paper under the tracing, and retrace the design using a stylus. We use gray and white graphite papers, gray on light backgrounds and white on dark backgrounds. If your graphite is new, wipe it with a paper towel to remove some graphite. After your painting is dry, erase any visible graphite lines with a soft white eraser before you varnish the project.

Chapter Two

Techniques

Prepare and Finish the Surface

Surface Preparation

The surface preparation is very important to the finished look of the project. Check your wood piece for areas that need sanding.

How to Basecoat

Load your basecoating brush fully with acrylic paint. We prefer to use foam brushes because they basecoat without the ridges that bristle brushes leave. They wash out easily and are inexpensive enough to throw away. Apply the paint generously in the middle of your surface, then brush the paint over the rest of the surface and to the outside edges. By beginning your basecoat in the middle, you will less likely create a buildup of paint on the edges of the surface. Brush the basecoat color on quickly, and do not overstroke the wet paint once it begins to dry. Let the paint dry completely before applying a second layer of basecoat or tracing on a pattern. Apply at least two coats of the basecoat color, sanding between coats.

How to Varnish

To finish a project, we recommend either J.W. Etc. Satin Varnish or Delta Ceramcoat Satin Varnish. One problem people have with varnishing is the ridges from the brush's side. Our tip for this problem is to use a large mop brush. It does not have straight sides, thus does not create ridges. Do not purchase an expensive brush for this job; a cheaper brush does just as well. Wash the brush before the first use to remove any loose hairs. If your mop brush has loose hairs, wrap a piece of masking tape around one hand and stroke your mop brush lightly over the tape. The tape will gently remove any loose hairs.

Tape Out Inserts

Make painting inserts easy by pressing a quality transparent tape along the

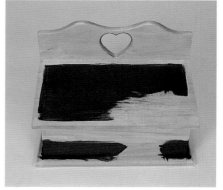

edges of your insert area. Smooth the tape down with your finger to ensure a tight bond with the wood surface. Brush on your basecoat, slightly overlapping the inside edge of the transparent tape. Let the first layer dry and apply a second layer before you remove the tape. Pull the tape toward the painted insert when you remove it so any wet paint on the tape will be pulled into the insert.

How to Faux Finish a Box

Step 1

Using a large flat brush and acrylic extender medium, generously dampen the flat top of the box. Move to step two immediately.

Step 2

Using a large flat brush, quickly and loosely slip-slap the following three colors on the surface: Antique Rose, Violet Haze, White. Move to step three immediately.

Step 3

Use a dry, rounded, fine-textured sponge to blend the colors, starting from the center and working out to the edges. The extender will lengthen your open time, but you still need to work quickly to soften and slightly blend the colors together. Pounce up and down with the dry sponge on top of the lid, mixing the colors together as you blend your way across the top of the box. Let this dry completely before faux finishing the side of the lid.

Antiquing

Step 1

Allow the finished piece to dry completely. Erase any visible pattern lines.

Step 2

Varnish the completed art with one layer of acrylic varnish. Let dry completely. We prefer to use large mop brushes to apply the varnish because you can apply a large amount of varnish, yet the brushes leave no ridges of varnish behind.

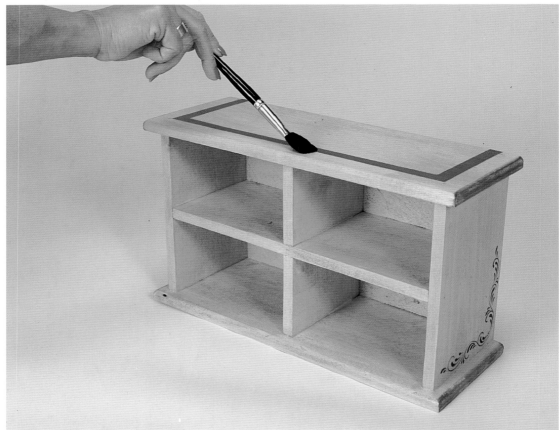

Painting Blooms and Blossoms

Step 3

Moisten the area you will be antiquing with a scant layer of odorless mineral spirits applied with a soft cloth. Using Winsor & Newton Burnt Umber oil paint and a soft cloth, rub a generous amount of oil paint on the edges of the surface. Rub well on the cut edges and work the oil paint into the wood grain.

Step 4

Soften and blend the oil paint on the surface using a clean, soft cloth. We prefer to use oil paint because it imparts a warm, rich antique look to wooden surfaces. Let the oil paint dry completely before finishing the varnish procedure with two to three more layers of acrylic varnish.

FOLK ART FLOWERS BIRDHOUSE

This first project starts with the basis of most decorative painting: strokework. Using some basic strokes, we have designed a delightful springtime birdhouse. Once you have tried these various flower forms, we think you will have fun painting them on a variety of projects. One suggestion is to paint the flowers around the bottom of a round box with the top plaided in the colors used in the flowers. Several examples of plaid appear in this book for you to try. The design given covers the front and side of the birdhouse. Repeat the pattern for the back and other side, or use the design to make any arrangement of the flowers you wish.

Materials Needed

Brushes
nos. 6/0, 10/0 script liner
nos. 2, 4, 6, 8 flat
no. 3 round
no. 1 liner

Wood Source
Copper roof birdhouse by Art Crafters, 525 Park Ave., Lafayette, IN 47904-3256

Additional Supplies
Small round sponge
Stylus
Graphite paper
Tracing paper

Paint: D = Delta Ceramcoat; DA = DecoArt Americana

White (D)

Crocus Yellow (D)

Burnt Sienna (DA)

Pink Frosting (D)

Spice Pink (DA)

Raspberry (DA)

Summer Lilac (DA)

Pansy Lavender (DA)

Blue Heaven (D)

Blueberry (D)

Village Green (D)

Wedgewood Green (D)

Green Sea (D)

Forest Green (D)

Dark Forest Green (D)

Mix—Forest Green + Green Sea (1:1)

Mix—Blue Heaven + Blueberry (1:1)

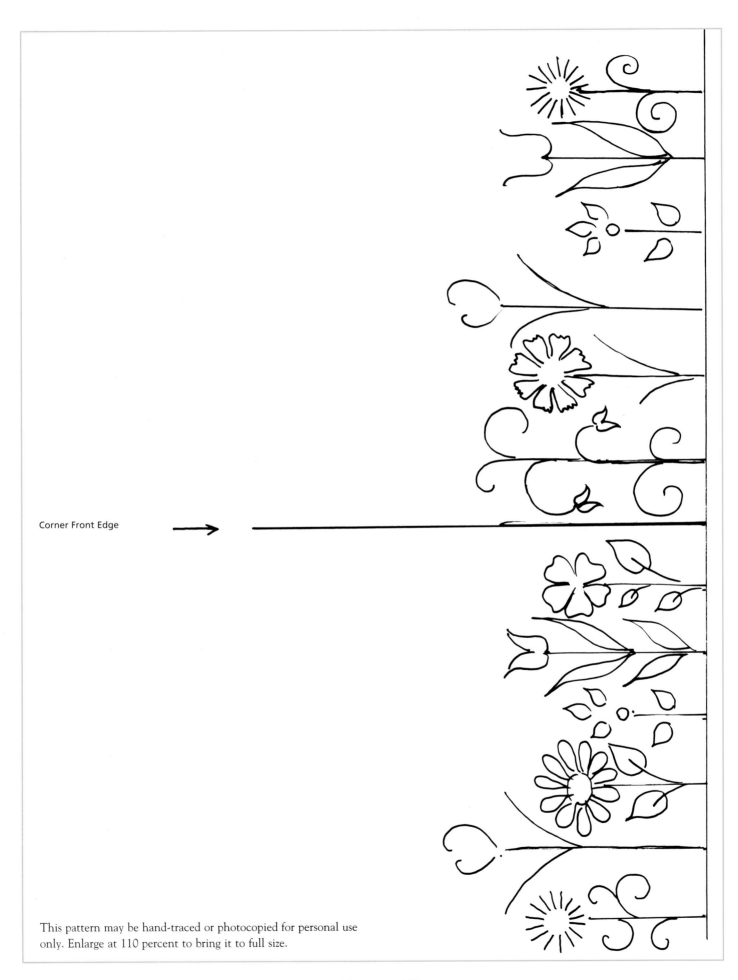

Corner Front Edge

This pattern may be hand-traced or photocopied for personal use only. Enlarge at 110 percent to bring it to full size.

Painting Blooms and Blossoms

1 BASECOAT THE BIRDHOUSE

Basecoat the birdhouse with a mix of Winter Blue and White (1:1).

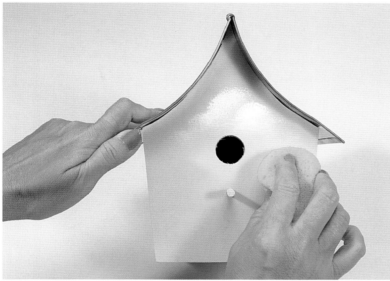

2 SPONGE IN THE CLOUDS

Using a small round sponge with a small amount of White paint on one edge, lightly tap in the tops of the clouds. Softly streak the White to form the bottoms of the clouds.

SPONGING THE CLOUDS, STEP BY STEP

3 PAINT THE STEMS

4 PAINT THE LEAVES

PAINT THE FLOWERS

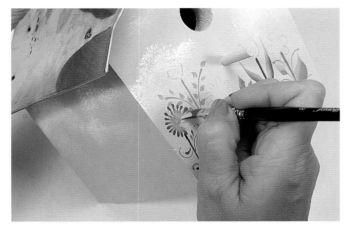

5 THE ASTERS

Paint the stems, tendrils and one-stroke leaves of the asters using a 6/0 liner loaded with Forest Green. Double-load a no. 8 flat brush with Summer Lilac and Pansy Lavender. With the light color to the center of the flower, stand on the chisel edge of the brush and slightly push the brush in the direction of the darker color. Paint each petal this way. Paint the center of the flower with dots of Crocus Yellow.

ASTER FLOWERS, STEP BY STEP

6 THE COMMA STROKE FLOWERS, STEP BY STEP

Paint the stems using a 6/0 liner loaded with Wedgewood Green. Using a no. 2 flat brush, paint the leaves with one-strokes of Wedgewood Green. Paint the flower petals with a double-loaded no. 4 flat brush with White and Crocus Yellow. Start with two petals in the center, then do the two side petals, finishing with the smaller center stroke. The dot at the base of the flower is Pansy Lavender.

7 THE DAISIES, STEP BY STEP

Paint the stems of the daisies with thin lines of Forest Green. Paint the leaves using a no. 8 flat brush double-loaded with Forest Green and Green Sea. Now paint the one-stroke leaves. Paint the stems of the leaves with Forest Green. Using a no. 3 round brush, stroke in the daisy petals with White. Paint the daisy center with Crocus Yellow, and shade at the bottom and in the center hollow with Burnt Sienna. Paint the dots around the center with Burnt Sienna.

8 THE DOT FLOWERS, STEP BY STEP

Use a no. 4 flat brush to paint the one-stroke leaves and the stems with a mix of Forest Green + Green Sea (1:1). The dots can be made with the end of your brush. Paint the dot petals with Spice Pink and the large center dot with Crocus Yellow.

9 BASECOAT THE LEAVES AND TULIPS

Paint the tulip stems with thin lines of Dark Forest Green. Paint the leaves with long strokes of Dark Forest Green and Village Green double-loaded on a no. 6 flat brush. Start on the chisel edge of the brush. Apply pressure to make the main portion of the leaf, and end on the chisel edge of the brush to finish the leaf. Basecoat the tulip with Pink Frosting. Shade the bottom curves of the tulip with a side-load float of Raspberry using a no. 8 flat brush.

10 OVERSTROKES ON THE TULIPS

Overstroke the tops of the tulip petals with White using a no. 1 liner. Make the stamens coming from the center of the tulip with fine lines and dots of Raspberry.

THE PINK TULIPS, STEP BY STEP

11 THE BLUE PETAL FLOWERS, STEP BY STEP

Paint the stems and tendrils with thin lines of Green Sea. Paint the leaves with double-loaded one strokes using a no. 8 flat brush with Green Sea and Village Green. Paint the petals with a double-loaded stroke of White and Blue Heaven. Stand a no. 8 flat brush on the chisel edge. Flatten the brush to the side and wiggle the brush slightly to achieve some curves to the petal top. Finish the petal by returning to the chisel edge. Double-load a no. 4 flat brush with Raspberry and White. With the White at the center of the flower and the brush on the chisel edge, tap in the center stamens of the flower. Outline the flower petals with a very thin line using a mix of Blue Heaven + Blueberry (1:1).

12 THE BLEEDING HEART STROKE FLOWERS, STEP BY STEP

Paint the stems, tendrils and strokes with a 6/0 liner loaded with a mix of Forest Green and Green Sea (1:1). Make the flowers with two strokes of Raspberry using a no. 3 round brush. Overstroke the petals using a 6/0 liner loaded with White, and paint the stamens and dots with Raspberry using a 6/0 liner.

13 THE BLUE CORNFLOWERS
Paint the stems of the cornflowers with Forest Green. Make the leaves with double-loaded one strokes of Forest Green and Village Green using a no. 4 flat brush. Paint the cornflower with a double-loaded stroke of White and Blue Heaven. Use a no. 8 flat brush, wiggling it back and forth on the chisel edge to create each petal. Paint the center with a double-loaded chisel stroke of White and Crocus Yellow. Stand on the edge of the chisel and tap in the flower stamens. Add a few more chisel strokes with Burnt Sienna added to the yellow end of the brush.

THE BLUE CORNFLOWERS, STEP BY STEP

Painting Blooms and Blossoms

PAINT THE FOLIAGE, GRASSES AND LEAVES

14 THE BASE FOLIAGE
With a small round sponge, using any green from your palette, lightly sponge around the bottom of the birdhouse to create the base foliage. This foliage should fluctuate in height, but should never be more than 1″ (2.54cm) tall.

15 THE GRASSES
Using a 10/0 liner and any of the greens on your palette, add some fine grasses around the base of the birdhouse.

16 THE GRASS SEEDS
With your stylus and any of the greens on your palette, add some grass seeds to some of the grasses.

17 THE WHITE DOTS
Using your stylus, add some dots of White to some of the grasses. This adds another touch of brightness and looseness to the design.

FOLIAGE, GRASSES, LEAVES AND DOTS, STEP BY STEP

FINISHED BIRDHOUSE, SIDE VIEW

FINISHED BIRDHOUSE, FRONT VIEW

Painting Blooms and Blossoms

COMPLETE THE BIRDHOUSE
Allow the project to dry completely. Erase
any visible graphite lines. Varnish with
three coats of acrylic varnish.

ASTERS ON A BASKET LID

Painting asters is an excellent way to practice your one strokes and paint pretty flowers at the same time. The asters are painted as layers of one-strokes starting with the darkest color value and working up the value scale to the top petals on the aster. Finish painting your flowers with an easy-to-paint, fluffy flower center.

Materials Needed

Brushes
no. 3 round
no. 1 liner
nos. 4, 8, 10 flat
small stipple brush

Wood Source
Pesky Bear

Additional Supplies
Krylon Crystal Clear Acrylic Spray
Acrylic varnish

Paint: D = Delta Ceramcoat; DA = DecoArt Americana

White (D)

Taffy Cream (DA)

Sand (D)

Golden Brown (D)

Burnt Umber (D)

Burnt Sienna (DA)

Eggshell (DA)

English Yew (D)

Black Green (DA)

Raspberry (DA)

Deep Burgundy (DA)

Black Plum (DA)

Mix—Deep Burgundy
+ Black Plum (1:1)

Mix—Raspberry +
White (3:1)

Mix—Raspberry
+ White (1:1)

Mix—White + a touch
of Raspberry

Mix: Eggshell +
English Yew +
Black Green (2:1:½)

This pattern may be hand-traced or photo-copied for personal use only. Enlarge at 100 percent to bring it to full size.

Painting Blooms and Blossoms

1 BASECOAT THE LID

Basecoat the basket lid with two coats of Eggshell. Let dry completely, then sand lightly between coats. I find it easier to paint the design with the knob removed from the basket lid.

PAINT THE LEAVES AND VINES

2 THE MAIN LEAVES

Use a no. 8 flat brush double-loaded heavily with English Yew and Sand. Overblend the colors until the Sand turns to a soft green shade. Begin the main stroke leaf at the base, keeping the Sand edge toward the outside edge of the leaf. Paint half of the leaf at a time. To paint the leaf apply pressure to the brush, flattening out the bristles. Then slide the brush side-to-side, creating the ripples of the leaf. As you make the side-to-side motion, move the brush down one side of the leaf beginning horizontally and slowly pivoting to the chisel edge of the brush as you slide your way to the tip of the leaf. Repeat for the opposite side of the leaf, allowing the paint to overlap in the middle.

3 THE SHADOW LEAVES

Using a no. 8 flat brush loaded with thinned Black Plum, paint very sheer shadow leaves sparingly along the vine, varying the size. They become smaller the farther they are from the center of the design.

4 THE VINES

Using a liner brush loaded with thinned Burnt Umber, pull loose vining lines on the design and attach the main leaves. Hold the brush back on the handle, and roll the brush slowly back and forth between your fingers as you pull the vining lines. This will create loose, natural vines. Still using the liner brush and thinned Burnt Umber, paint vein lines on the main stroke leaves.

PAINT THE ASTERS

ASTER PETALS AND CENTER, STEP BY STEP

Since it is hard to paint background shading around the fluffy edges of the asters, I painted the two side asters first, applied the background shading, then, painted the center aster.

5 THE ASTER PETALS
Using a no. 3 round brush, paint the first layer of aster petals using a mix of Deep Burgundy + a touch of Black Plum. Paint the first layer with one strokes on the "clock marks" at one, three, six, nine and twelve. Finish this layer of petals by painting two additional one strokes between each clock mark. Paint the second layer of petals with Raspberry. Paint one stroke between each stroke on the first layer. Paint the third layer of petals with a mix of Raspberry + a touch of White (enough White to see a slight value change). When you paint the third layer of petals, place them randomly around the circle, slightly shorter than the first and second layer. Paint the fourth layer using the third layer mix plus more White.

❧ **HINT** ❧ *I like to brush mix as I paint the fourth layer so some petals are whiter than others. Variety is good!*

Paint the fourth layer of one-stroke petals within the highlight section of the aster. Paint the partial blossoms using strokes in the colors of the first, second and/or third layers of petal colors.

6 THE ASTER CENTERS
Using a small stipple brush, basecoat the centers with Golden Brown. While still damp, shade one side with a stipple of Burnt Sienna and highlight the opposite side with a stipple of Taffy Cream. Using the tip of the liner brush, paint very small dots of Black Plum around the shaded half of the flower center, and highlight with small dots of Taffy Cream.

❧ **HINT** ❧ *Notice how some dots are on the flower center and some spill over onto the flower petals. This creates a loose, fluffy look to the flower centers.*

7 SHADE THE ASTERS

Using a large flat brush corner-loaded sparingly with Black Plum, softly side-load float around the perimeter of the main aster circle on top of the side asters. This step creates a soft background shading behind the center aster. Using the same brush, tint the outside edges of several main leaves with a soft side-load float of Black Plum.

8 PAINT THE CENTER ASTER

Paint the center aster using the same colors and steps as the aster petals and centers. It has to be done at this time because of the shading underneath.

9 PAINT THE CALYXES AND FILLER LEAVES

On the larger partial flowers, paint the calyxes as three small one-stroke leaves using a no. 4 flat brush double-loaded with English Yew and Black Green. On the smaller partial flowers, paint the calyxes as thin lines in a brush mix of English Yew + a touch of Black Green. Using a no. 4 flat brush and a mix of Black Green and English Yew (1:1), paint small one-stroke filler leaves sparingly along the vine and tucked next to the main asters.

❧ **HINT** ❧ *Careful, it's easy to paint too many of the filler leaves which results in a crowded design.*

PAINT THE STROKEWORK BORDER

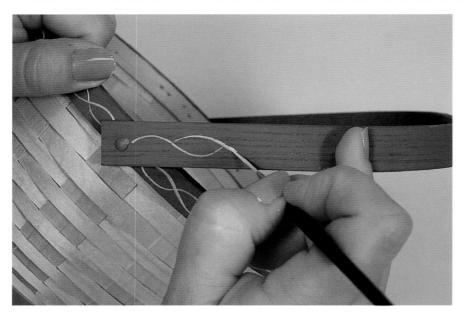

10 BASECOAT THE BASKET RIM AND HANDLE

Basecoat the basket handle and rim with a mix of Eggshell + English Yew + Black Green (1:2:½).

11 THE STROKEWORK TRIM

Using a liner brush and slightly thinned Eggshell paint the strokework border as intersecting lines. Begin each strokework line on the tip of the liner brush, apply slight pressure in the middle of the stroke, then release back to the tip of the liner brush to finish the stroke. You may wish to draw a center chalk line and mark the line with a 1.5″ (3.8cm) increments to aid in positioning the strokework trim.

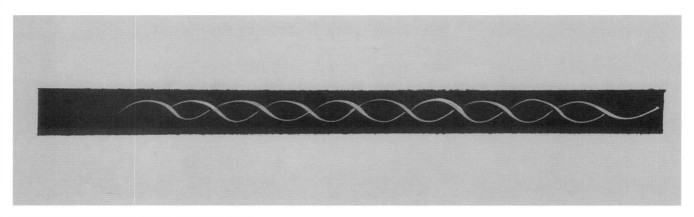

THE STROKEWORK BORDER, STEP BY STEP

12 FINISH YOUR PROJECT
Varnish the lid, rim and handle of the basket with two to three layers of your favorite acrylic varnish. Apply one layer of Krylon Crystal Clear Acrylic Spray on the woven portion of the basket.

3 FLOWERING HERB PLATE

A few years ago I removed the grass from my backyard and replaced it with a walking perennial garden. I have herbs around the outside of my patio for convenient clippings. Their aroma adds to the pleasure of sitting on the patio. I am certainly no expert on herbs, but I do enjoy cooking with them. I have noticed I have added them to several of my recent paintings because they are close at hand. Always paint what you know and see. I hope you will enjoy painting this plate and try a little herb gardening for yourself.

Materials Needed

Brushes
nos. 2, 4, 6, 8, 10, 12 flat
#480 series—nos. 1, 6/0, 10/0
#455 series—no. 1 liner
½-inch (1.3cm) rake

Wood Source
12″ (30.5cm) wood plate with 2″ (5.1cm) rim with one bead between center and rim
Wayne's Woodenware

Additional Supplies
Ruler
Chalk pencil

Paints: D = Delta Ceramcoat; DA = DecoArt Americana

Khaki Tan (DA)

White (D)

Light Buttermilk (DA)

Spice Brown (D)

Dark Forest Green (D)

Forest Green (D)

Wedgewood Green (D)

Shale Green (DA)

Pansy Lavender (DA)

Royal Purple (DA)

Dioxazine Purple (DA)

Antique Rose (D)

French Mauve (DA)

Golden Straw (DA)

Jade Green (DA)

Mix—Forest Green + Wedgewood Green (1:1)

Mix—Khaki Tan + White (1:1)

Mix—Khaki Tan mix + more White (1:1)

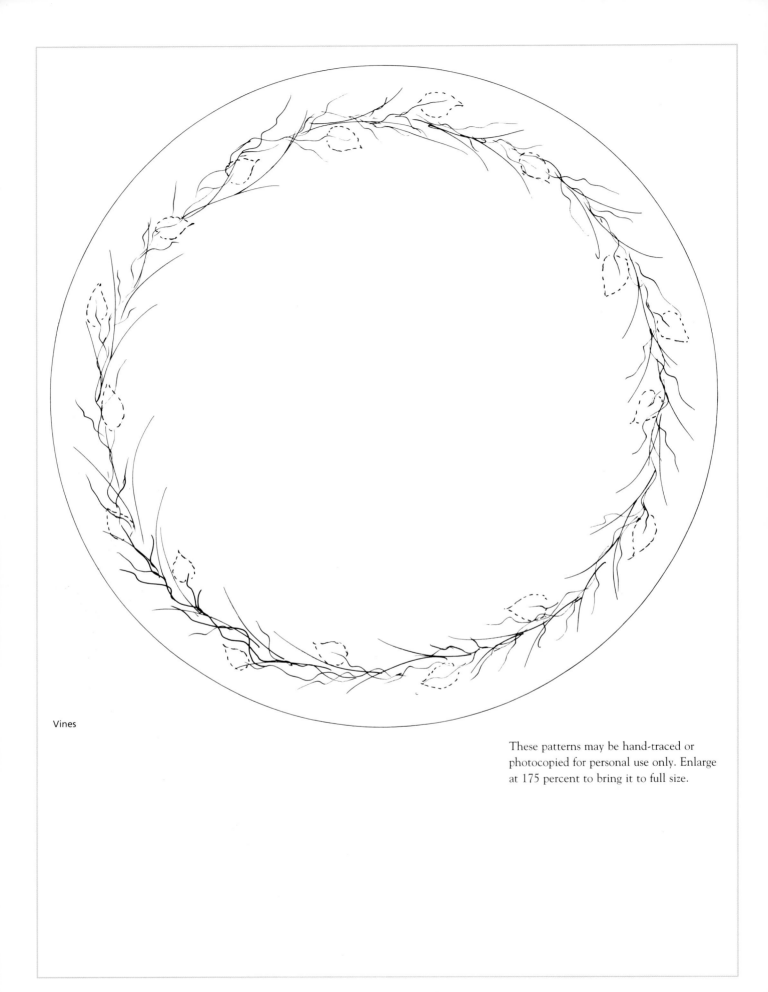

Vines

These patterns may be hand-traced or photocopied for personal use only. Enlarge at 175 percent to bring it to full size.

Painting Blooms and Blossoms

Herbs

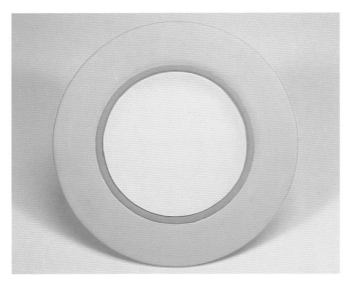

1 BASECOAT THE PLATE

Basecoat the outside rim of the plate with a mix of Khaki Tan and White (1:1) Basecoat the inside circle of the plate with the previous mix plus more White (1:1) Basecoat the inner rim with a mix of one part Pansy Lavender, one part Shale Green and a touch of White.

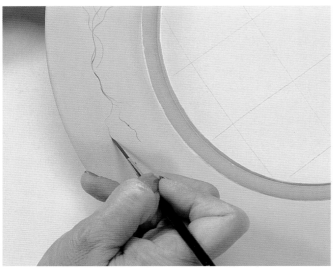

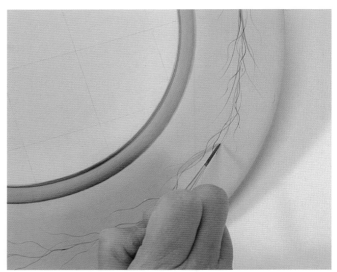

2 PAINT THE VINES

Paint the vines with very thin, irregular lines in the center of the rim, 1″ (2.54cm) from the outside edge. Use a no. 1 liner brush loaded with Spice Brown. Then add a few more vines with Dark Forest Green.

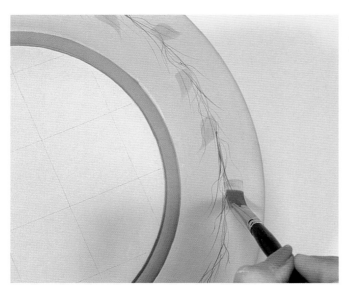

3 PAINT THE SHADOW LEAVES

Paint the shadow one-stroke leaves with a no. 12 flat brush loaded with a thinned mix of Forest Green + Shale Green (1:1).

PAINT THE LAVENDER

4 STEMS AND LEAVES
Paint the stems using a no. 1 liner brush loaded with Wedgewood Green. Paint the leaves with a brush mix of Wedgewood Green and Shale Green using the no. 1 liner brush. Occasionally, touch your brush in Forest Green to have a variety of leaf colors.

5 THE LAVENDER FLOWERS
Create the flowers with groupings of very small C-strokes. Use a no. 2 flat brush double-loaded with White and Pansy Lavender, White and Dioxazine Purple or a combination of the purples.

STEMS, LEAVES AND FLOWERS, STEP BY STEP

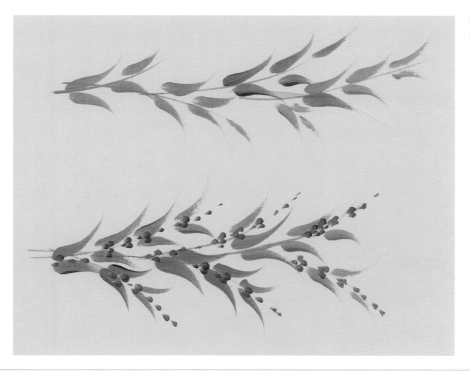

PAINT THE CHAMOMILE

6 THE STEMS AND LEAVES
Paint the stems and one-stroke leaves with Forest Green using a no. 1 liner brush.

7 THE CHAMOMILE FLOWERS
Paint the flowers with small daisy petal strokes of White. This flower looks like a tiny daisy. Paint the center with Golden Straw and shade along the bottom edge with Spice Brown.

STEMS, LEAVES AND FLOWERS,
STEP BY STEP

Painting Blooms and Blossoms

PAINT THE OREGANO

8 THE STEMS AND LEAVES
Paint the stems of the oregano with a mix of Forest Green and Spice Brown (2:1). Paint the large leaves using a no. 8 flat brush double-loaded with Forest Green and Jade Green. Paint the leaves in two strokes with the Forest Green to the outside of the leaf. Use Dark Forest Green for the veins in the large leaves. Paint the small one-stroke leaves using a no. 4 flat brush double-loaded with Forest Green and Spice Brown. You may also touch into Khaki Tan for some variety.

9 THE OREGANO FLOWERS
Paint the flowers with dabs of brush-mixed Antique Rose and White. Use small strokes of Dark Forest Green for the calyxes at the flower's base.

STEMS, LEAVES AND FLOWERS, STEP BY STEP

PAINT THE WINTER SAVORY

STEMS, LEAVES AND FLOWERS, STEP BY STEP

10 THE STEMS AND LEAVES
Paint the stems and leaves using a no. 1 liner brush loaded with Dark Forest Green.

11 THE WINTER SAVORY FLOWERS
Paint the flowers with an oval C-stroke using a no. 1 round brush double-loaded with Pansy Lavender and Royal Purple. If the flowers seem too dark, add some White to the Pansy Lavender. Create stamens coming out of the flowers with a mix of Pansy Lavender + Royal Purple (1:1) using a no. 5/0 liner brush. Paint the calyxes with Forest Green.

PAINT THE EVENING PRIMROSE

12 THE STEMS AND LEAVES
Paint the stems with Wedgewood Green. Paint the leaves with double-loaded one strokes of Forest Green and Wedgewood Green using a no. 8 flat brush. Make the veins with Forest Green and a touch of Dark Forest Green.

13 THE EVENING PRIMROSE FLOWERS
Paint the flowers with a large double-loaded C-stroke of White and Golden Straw using a no. 4 flat brush with the yellow to the outside of the petal. Paint with a brush mix of Golden Straw and a touch of Spice Brown. Use the previous mix plus more Spice Brown for the stamens coming out of the center.

STEMS, LEAVES AND FLOWERS, STEP BY STEP

PAINT THE THYME

STEMS, LEAVES AND FLOWERS, STEP BY STEP

14 THE STEMS AND LEAVES
Paint the stems and leaves with a thinned paint mix of Forest Green and Wedgewood Green (1:1), using a no. 4 flat brush. Paint the center veins into the leaves with Forest Green.

15 THE THYME FLOWERS
Using a no. 1 liner or round brush, brush mix French Mauve and Antique Rose with a touch of White for the flowers. Paint the flowers as small dabs in groups of two or three between the leaf and stem.

PAINT THE PLAID

16 THE LARGE STRIPE
The large plaid stripes are 1¾″ (4.4cm) apart. Use a ½″ (1.3cm) or no. 12 flat brush loaded with a very thin paint mix of Khaki Tan and White (1:1) This is the same color as the plate rim.

17 THE THIN KHAKI STRIPE
To the right of each broad stripe, paint a thin stripe of Khaki Tan using a no. 5/0 liner brush. This is about ⅛″ (0.3cm) from the broad stripe.

18 THE LIGHT BUTTERMILK STRIPES
About ⅛″ (0.3cm) from the thin Khaki Tan stripe and to the left of the broad stripe, paint a thin stripe of Light Buttermilk with the same brush used previously.

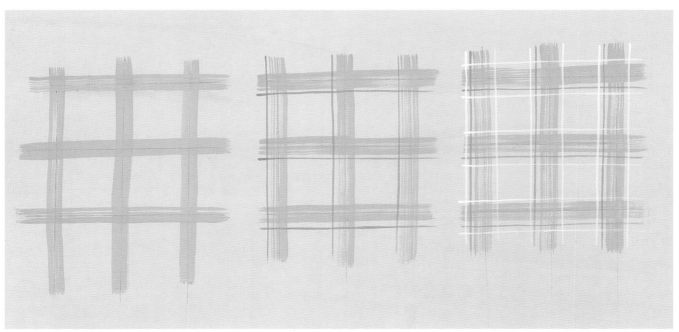

PLAID STRIPES, STEP BY STEP

19 FINISH THE FLOWERING HERB PLATE

Allow your piece to dry thoroughly. Erase any visible graphite lines and varnish with three coats of acrylic varnish.

APPLE BLOSSOM TIME

When Lynne and I were deciding what flowers to feature in this book, we realized there were several patterns for dogwood, but none for apple blossoms. Since the apple blossom is the state flower of Michigan, our home state, we felt it was fitting we feature an apple blossom box in our book.

Paint: D = Delta Ceramcoat; DA = DecoArt Americana

Materials Needed

Brushes
nos. 10/0, 6/0, 1 liner
nos. 2, 4, 6, 8, 10, 12 flat
¾-inch (1.9cm) rake

Wood Source
Woodcrafts

Additional Supplies
Old toothbrush
Ruler
Chalk pencil

White (D)

Light Buttermilk (DA)

Buttermilk (DA)

Cool Neutral (DA)

Driftwood (DA)

Khaki Tan (DA)

Raw Sienna (D)

Sable Brown (DA)

Burnt Umber (D)

Charcoal Grey (DA)

Crocus Yellow (DA)

Cadmium Yellow (DA)

Olive Green (DA)

Hauser Medium Green (DA)

Forest Green (D)

Hauser Dark Green (DA)

Rose Petal Pink (D)

Wild Rose (D)

Mix—Khaki Tan + Burnt Umber (1:1)

Mix—Olive Green + Forest Green + Cool Neutral (1:1:1)

Mix—Hauser Medium Green + Forest Green (1:1)

Mix—Hauser Dark Green + Forest Green (1:1)

Mix—Olive Green + Light Buttermilk + Cool Neutral (1:1)

Mix—Rose Petal Pink + Wild Rose (1:1)

Mix—Olive Green + Hauser Medium Green + Cool Neutral (1:1:1)

Mix—Hauser Medium Green + Cool Neutral + Charcoal Grey (1:1:1)

Painting Blooms and Blossoms

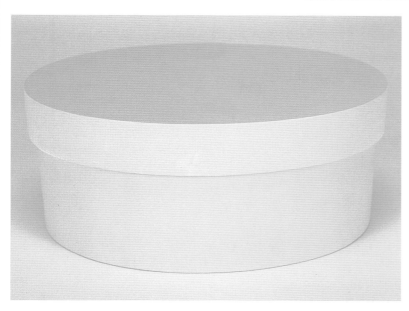

1 BASECOAT THE BOX
Basecoat the box with a mix of Khaki Tan and Buttermilk (1:1).

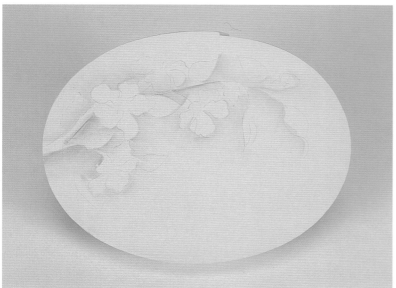

2 SHADE THE BACKGROUND
First, apply the pattern. Shade around the outside edge of the major flowers and the branch with a very soft side-load float of Sable Brown. Use a 1-inch (2.54cm) brush for a softer float.

3 FLY-SPECKING
Using an old toothbrush (no, do not borrow your husband's), fly-speck the top of the box with Sable Brown with a touch of Burnt Umber. Fly-speck the heaviest around the main part of the design.

4 PAINT THE BRANCHES

Using a no. 1 round brush loaded with Driftwood, begin stroking in the main branches. Using a no. 12 flat brush, overstroke the branch from the bottom up with Charcoal Grey. Using a no. 12 flat brush, overstroke the branch from the top down with Cool Neutral or Cool Neutral and a touch of White. With a 10/0 liner brush add some detail lines on the branches with Charcoal Grey and Cool Neutral. Complete the ends of the branches with fine lines of Charcoal Grey.

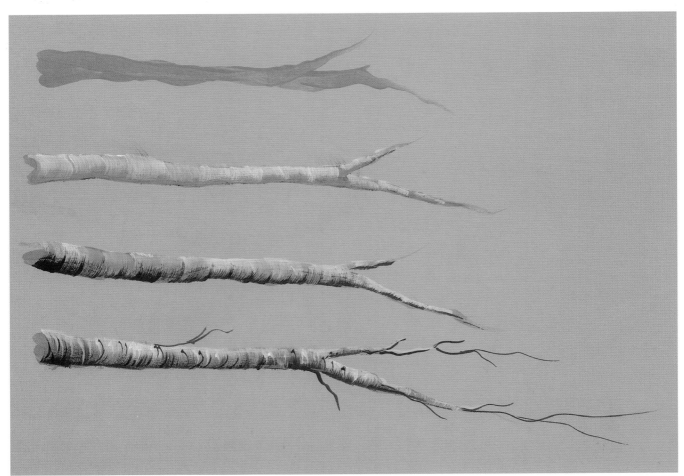

THE BRANCHES, STEP BY STEP

Painting Blooms and Blossoms

5 PAINT THE LEAVES

Paint the lighter shadow leaves with a thinned mix of Olive Green + Forest Green + Driftwood (1:1:1). Overstroke these leaves with Cool Neutral using a no. 10 flat brush. Paint the veins with a mix of Sable Brown + Charcoal Grey (1:1). Basecoat the main leaves with a mix of Hauser Medium Green + Forest Green (1:1). Overstroke the main leaves with Olive Green, a brush mix of Olive Green and Cool Neutral, or a brush mix of Olive Green and Light Buttermilk using a no. 12 flat brush. Shade the bottom and center of the leaf using a no. 8 flat brush loaded with Hauser Dark Green + Forest Green (1:1).

HINT *You may deepen these mixes with a touch of Charcoal Grey.*

Highlight the leaf edges with a float of Olive Green + Light Buttermilk + Cool Neutral (1:1:1). Highlight the veins in the leaves with the same mix. Tint some of the leaves with a soft float of Wild Rose. You may deepen the Wild Rose by adding a touch of Charcoal Grey. Paint the added tendrils using a 10/0 liner with a brush mix of Charcoal Grey, Burnt Umber and Sable Brown.

THE LEAVES, STEP BY STEP

6 PAINT THE APPLE BLOSSOMS

Basecoat the petals with Buttermilk. Shade the petals using a no. 6 flat brush double-loaded with Buttermilk and a mix of Rose Petal Pink + Wild Rose (1:1). Highlight the outside edges with a float of White.

7 PAINT THE APPLE BLOSSOM CENTERS

Paint the stamens with thin lines using a 10/0 liner loaded with Crocus Yellow. Deepen the base of the stamen lines with a touch of Raw Sienna. Paint the pollen tops of the stamens with dashes of Crocus Yellow + Buttermilk (1:1) Use a brush mix of Hauser Medium Green and Cool Neutral for the green center dots.

THE APPLE BLOSSOMS, STEP BY STEP

Painting Blooms and Blossoms

8 PAINT THE FILLER BLOSSOMS AND LEAVES

Paint the filler blossoms with small C-strokes. Using a no. 4 flat brush loaded with a mix of Rose Petal Pink + Wild Rose (1:1), create the little filler blossoms. Paint the filler leaves with a mix of Olive Green + Hauser Medium Green + Cool Neutral (1:1:1). Using a no. 8 flat brush with the above mixture thinned, paint little one-stroke leaves. Then, shade next to some of the loose tendrils with a float of Sable Brown.

PAINT THE PLAID

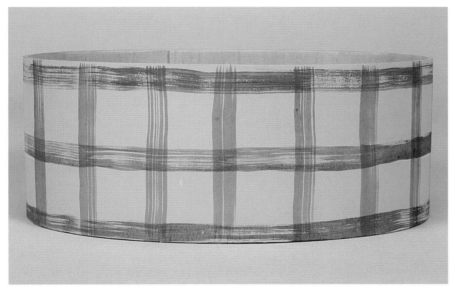

9 THE LARGE STRIPES

Paint the large stripes of the plaid 1½" (3.8cm) apart, using a ½-inch (1.3) rake brush or no. 12 flat brush. Paint the large stripes with a mix of Hauser Medium Green + Cool Neutral (1:1) with a touch of Charcoal Grey.

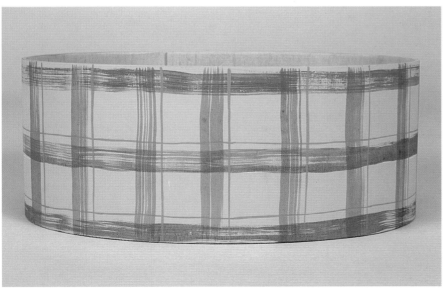

10 THE PINK STRIPE

About an eighth inch (0.3cm) away from the right or above the broad stripe, paint a thin stripe of the pink mix, Rose Petal Pink + Wild Rose (1:1) using a 10/0 liner brush.

11 THE LIGHT PINK STRIPE
About an eighth inch (0.3cm) from the pink stripes, paint a light pink stripe with Buttermilk added to the pink mix (1:1).

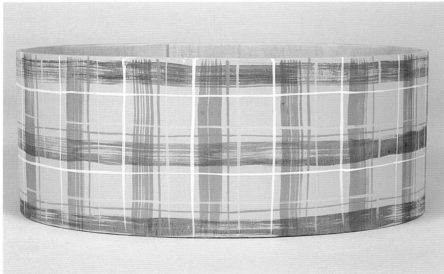

12 THE LIGHT STRIPE
About an ⅛″ from the left and below the broad stripe, do a light stripe of a mix of Buttermilk and White (1:1).

13 FINISH THE BOX
Allow the paint to dry completely. Erase any visible graphite lines and apply at least three coats of acrylic varnish.

The Finished Lid

PANSIES AND RIBBONS DRESSER BOX

F lats of colorful pansies at the local nursery in the springtime . . . what a glorious sight! Pansies are one of my favorite flowers to paint, probably because they are so colorful and delicate, yet so easy. Follow the step-by-step instructions to "welcome spring" into your home.

Materials Needed

Brushes
no. 1 liner
nos. 4, 8, 10, ½-inch (1.3cm), ¾-inch (1.9cm) flat

Wood Source
Wooden dresser box from Wayne's Woodenware

Additional Supplies
Acrylic varnish
Paper doily place mats

Paint: D = Delta Ceramcoat; DA = DecoArt Americana

Antique White (D)

Pale Yellow (D)

Desert Sand (DA)

Yellow Ochre (DA)

Honey Brown (DA)

Ocean Mist Blue (D)

Light Timberline (D)

Rainforest (D)

Forest Green (D)

Dark Forest Green (D)

Pink Parfait (D)

Lilac Dusk (D)

Antique Rose (D)

Dusty Mauve (D)

Black Cherry (D)

White (D)

Vintage Wine (D)

Payne's Grey (DA)

Black Green (DA)

Mix—Rainforest + Forest Green (1:1)

Spice Brown (D)

This pattern may be hand-traced or photo-copied for personal use only. Enlarge at 141 percent to bring it to full size.

BASECOAT THE LEAVES, RIBBON AND PANSY PETALS

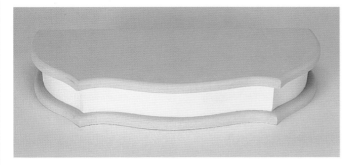

1 SURFACE PREPARATION
Basecoat the flat side of the dresser box with Antique White. Basecoat the lid and bottom (except for the center) of the dresser box with Desert Sand. Let dry completely, then sand lightly. Apply the pattern.

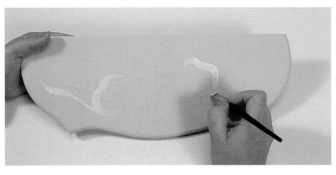

2 BASECOAT THE RIBBON, STEP 1
Using a no. 10 flat brush loaded with thinned White, stroke in the ribbon loops and ties. Basecoat each separate ribbon loop and tie as one continuous stroke to achieve a smooth layer of paint. Notice how the angle of the brush follows the curve of the ribbon loop.

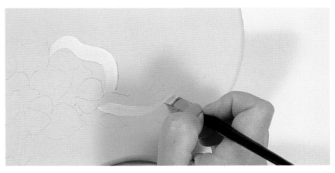

3 BASECOAT THE RIBBON, STEP 2
Notice the angle of the brush when basecoating the ribbon tie. Use the flat width of the brush to basecoat the fullest section of the ribbon tie, then slowly slide to the brush's chisel edge to bring the ribbon tie to a point.

4 THE MAIN LEAVES
Using a no. 10 flat brush and a mix of thinned Rainforest + Forest Green (1:1) corner-loaded into either Light Timberline or Ocean Mist Blue, basecoat all leaves. Keep the Light Timberline or Ocean Mist Blue edge of the brush to the leaf's outside edge. Basecoat each leaf using two opposite overlapping strokes. Paint only one layer, keeping the basecoat thin.

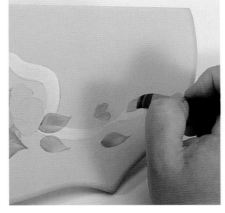

5 THE SMALLER LEAVES
Basecoat the smaller leaves in one stroke using a no. 10 flat brush and thinned paint. Just like the main leaves, use a mix of Rainforest + Forest Green (1:1) corner-loaded into Light Timberline or Ocean Mist Blue.
❧ HINT ❧ *Vary the colors to achieve variety in the design.*

6 THE PANSY PETALS
Basecoat the pansy petals using a no. 10 flat brush and sheer paint as you stroke in each petal. Basecoat the petal first using the chisel edge of the brush. Then, flatten the brush as you paint the fullest part of the pansy petal. Basecoat the white pansy petals using slightly thinned Antique White. Basecoat the yellow pansy petals with slightly thinned Yellow Ochre and the light pink pansy petals with slightly thinned Antique Rose. Basecoat the dark pink petals with slightly thinned Dusty Mauve.

SHADE THE RIBBON, LEAVES AND PANSY PETALS

7 THE RIBBON
Using a no. 10 flat brush corner-loaded with Rainforest, softly shade the ribbon loops and ties where they tuck behind the design.

8 FIRST SHADING ON THE LEAVES
Using a no. 10 flat brush corner-loaded into Dark Forest Green, softly shade each leaf. Notice in this picture how some leaves are shaded across the whole base of the leaf and some are shaded one-half at a time leaving a sliver of basecoat showing between the leaf halves. The result is a vein line down the center of those leaves.

❧ **H I N T** ❧ *Please notice when one leaf overlaps another, a sliver of basecoat shows through. This helps to define and separate the leaves and flower petals.*

9 FIRST SHADING ON THE PANSY PETALS
Shade all light pink and dark pink pansy petals with a soft side-load float of Honey Brown. Again, a sliver of basecoat is left unshaded between the pansy petals.

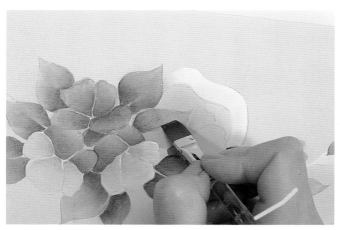

10 CREATE A VEIN ON THE LEAVES
First apply the shading color using the flat of the brush and pulling across the width of the leaf. When you are ready to establish the vein line, slide the chisel edge of the brush down the center area of the leaf. Shade the other half of the leaf in the same manner, leaving a sliver of basecoat showing between the two halves of the leaf.

11 A CLOSE-UP LOOK AT SHADING PANSY PETALS
Shade the width of the petals instead of from base to tip. Press the color down slightly away from the base of the petal, walking the color back into the V area. Then walk the brush out over the paint to widen the shaded area.

12 SECOND LAYER OF SHADING ON PINK PANSY PETALS
Using a no. 10 flat brush corner-loaded into a mix of Black Cherry + a touch of Payne's Grey, reinforce the first highlight area on all pink pansy petals. Maintain the petal separation lines.

13 SECOND LAYER OF SHADING ON LEAVES
Using a no. 10 flat brush corner-loaded sparingly into Black Green, reinforce the shaded areas on all leaves. Maintain the vein lines and leaf separations.

14 PAINT THE STEMS
Attach all leaves and partial blossoms to the main design with thin, nervous lines of Spice Brown. Thin the paint slightly to improve the paint flow. Pull several additional sections of loose vining from the design.

15 LEAF VEIN LINES
Using a liner brush and thinned Spice Brown, pull thin vein lines into each leaf. Pull side vein lines in the larger leaves and attach the smaller leaves with a single vein line.

16 SHADING LINES IN PANSY PETALS
Using a liner brush and thinned Vintage Wine, pull thin shading lines on the front three pansy petals. Begin each shading line at the petal's base and pull various line lengths into the petal's center.

17 HIGHLIGHT THE PINK PANSY PETALS, STEP 1
Using a ½-inch (1.3cm) or ¾-inch (1.9cm) flat brush corner-loaded heavily with Pink Parfait, side-load float along the outside edge of each light pink pansy petal. Highlight the outside edges of each dark pink pansy petal with a side-load float of Lilac Dusk. The corner of the brush is heavily loaded, so you'll need a generous amount of paint on the brush to create a strong highlight.

18 HIGHLIGHT THE PINK PANSY PETALS, STEP 2
Immediately after applying the highlight color, soften the paint into the center of the petal, and slightly overlap the ends of the shading lines.

19 HIGHLIGHT THE YELLOW AND WHITE PANSY PETALS, STEP 1
Using a ½-inch (1.3cm) or ¾-inch (1.9cm) flat brush corner-loaded into Pale Yellow, highlight the outside edge of each yellow pansy petal. Highlight the outside edge of each white pansy petal with a strong side-load float of White.

20 HIGHLIGHT THE YELLOW AND WHITE PANSY PETALS, STEP 2
Immediately after applying the highlight color, soften the paint into the center of the petal, and slightly overlap the ends of the shading lines. Notice how you can "ruffle" the highlight color along the outside edges of the pansy petals to create a loose look.

21 TINTS ON THE LEAVES
Using a large flat brush corner-loaded sparingly into Black Cherry, lightly tint the outside edges of some leaves. Just a little paint goes a long way!

22 THE FILLER LEAVES
Using a no. 4 flat brush loaded with a thinned mix of Rainforest + Forest Green (1:1), paint small one-stroke leaves sparingly along the stems and next to the main design. ❧ **H I N T** ☙ *Some of the filler leaves are painted in groups of threes. It makes for a nice grouping and really loosens the design.*

23 THE PANSY FLOWER CENTERS
Using a liner brush loaded with Pale Yellow, paint two small one strokes at the base of the three main petals in each pansy.

24 PARTIAL PANSY CALYXES
Using a liner brush loaded with Dark Forest Green, paint two nervous one strokes at the base of each partial pansy to create the calyx. Pull the stroke out a little farther than usual, creating a nervous finish line.

25 PAINT THE PIQUE EDGE ON THE RIBBON
Using a stylus and fresh White paint, dot uniformly along both edges of the ribbon loops and ties. ❧ **H I N T** ☙ *The dots decrease slightly in size when they are painted in the shade areas of the ribbon.*

26 SEPARATION SHADING ON PANSIES

Using a large flat brush corner-loaded sparingly into Payne's Grey, softly shade across any petals on the main three pansies that fall behind another pansy petal.

27 OUTLINE ON THE LID

Using a liner brush and a thinned mix of Rainforest + Forest Green (1:1), paint a thin line next to the scalloped edge of the box lid. Pull the brush toward you. While you paint the outline, look slightly ahead of your brush and paint with the tip.

THE LACE DOILY

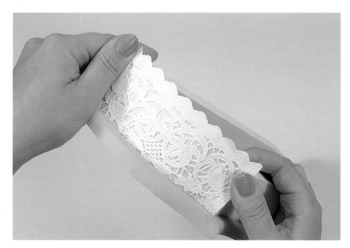

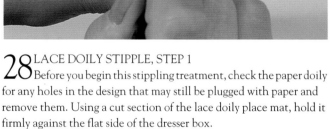

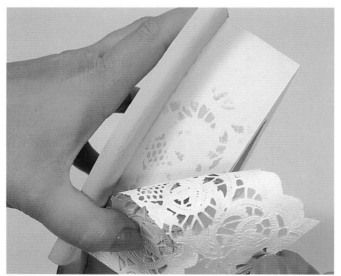

28 LACE DOILY STIPPLE, STEP 1

Before you begin this stippling treatment, check the paper doily for any holes in the design that may still be plugged with paper and remove them. Using a cut section of the lace doily place mat, hold it firmly against the flat side of the dresser box.

29 LACE DOILY STIPPLE, STEP 2

Load a dry stippler brush with Desert Sand. Pounce the loaded brush on a clean, dry paper towel to remove excess paint. Lightly stipple over the lace doily holes. Work a small section at a time, holding the lace doily firmly against the wooden surface.

30 LACE DOILY STIPPLE, STEP 3

Still holding the lace doily firmly against the wooden surface, pull back carefully to check that the design is completely stippled.

Painting Blooms and Blossoms

31 COMPLETE THE LACE DOILY STIPPLE
There are a wide variety of styles available in lace doilies, so have fun!

32 FINISH THE DRESSER BOX
Brush two to three layers of your favorite acrylic varnish on the inside and outside sections of the dresser box. Let the varnish cure twenty-four hours and sand lightly between coats. Don't forget to replace the hinges.

PASTEL POINSETTIA BOWL

This holiday bowl will look beautiful filled with pine-cones and holly, antique ornaments or winter fruits. For those of you who paint to sell, hand-painted wooden bowls always seem to be among the first items sold at craft shows. It seems people want to own decorative pieces that are lovely as well as functional. This project uses the "soft-float" painting technique which makes it easy to achieve wide shade and highlight areas.

Materials Needed

Brushes
6/0 liner
no. 3 round
nos. 4, 8, ½-inch (1.3cm), ¾-inch
    (1.9cm) flat

Wood Source
Wooden bowl from Holland Bowl Mill

Additional Supplies
Acrylic varnish
Old toothbrush

Paints: D = Delta Ceramcoat; DA = DecoArt Americana; A = Accent

White (D)

Light Ivory (D)

Sand (DA)

Pink Chiffon (DA)

Indiana Rose (D)

Dusty Rose (DA)

Antique Rose (D)

Deep Burgundy (DA)

Opaque Red (D)

Sable Brown (DA)

Blue Spruce (D)

Ocean Mist Blue (D)

Mushroom (A)

Olive Green (DA)

Rainforest (D)

Green Mist (DA)

Hauser Medium Green (DA)

Mix—Rainforest + Mushroom (1:1)

Mix—Blue Spruce + a touch of Deep Burgundy

Mix—Deep Burgundy + a touch of Blue Spruce

This pattern can be hand-traced or photo-copied for personal use only. Enlarge to 120 percent to bring it to full size.

Painting Blooms and Blossoms

1 SURFACE PREPARATION
Basecoat the inside and rim of the bowl with two layers of Blue Spruce. Let this dry completely and sand lightly between layers.

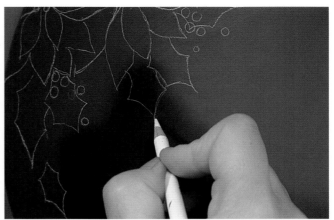

2 TRANSFER THE PATTERN
Break the pattern into smaller sections on tracing paper. Transfer one section at a time onto the bowl using worn graphite paper and a stylus. Use a chalk pencil to correct any pattern lines that became distorted in the transfer process.

BASECOAT THE FLOWERS AND LEAVES

3 STEP 1
Basecoat the white poinsettias with Sand and the pink poinsettias with Dusty Rose. Basecoat the number one holly leaves with Mushroom and the number two holly leaves with Green Mist.

⊰ HINT ⊱ *The basecoat on the poinsettias and holly leaves should look splotchy. It's OK. The object is to paint smooth layers of basecoat with no ridges. The position of the brush is important. Pull the brush toward you, shaping the outside edge of the holly leaf as you basecoat.*

4 STEP 2
Apply the second basecoat layer on the poinsettia and holly leaves. Don't worry if you go out of the pattern lines a little. It will easily clean up with a liner brush and the basecoat color when the bowl is completed.

THE SOFT-FLOAT TECHNIQUE

STEP 1

5 Dampen the area to be shaded or high-lighted with clear water.

❧ **H I N T** ❧ *Keep a small cup of clean water next to your water basin just for this purpose. Use a large flat brush to apply the water. The area should be moistened sparingly; you just want to see the surface glisten. If you apply too much water, the paint will repel against the edge of the object, creating a hard line. If you use too little water, the paint will drag on the surafce. Keep one brush on the side for wetting only. It saves on rinsing time.*

STEP 2

6 Use a large flat brush corner-loaded heav-ily with the appropriate shade or highlight color, and firmly apply the paint slightly away from the edge of the leaf or flower petal. Walk the paint back to the edge by pit-patting the brush over the paint. You have time to do this. The water on the surface slows the dry-ing time of the paint and helps diffuse it over the surface. The results are a soft shade or highlight. The width of the large flat brush allows the color to blend softly.

STEP 3

7 Once you have the surface moistened and applied the color, use a dry mop brush to soften the color. The mop brush should be used as a stipple brush, stippling very softly over the wet paint. Dry the mop brush frequently on a clean paper towel or a terry towel. Once you perfect this technique, it goes quickly and creates soft shades and highlights.

8 FIRST COLOR SHADING

Using the soft-float technique, apply one to two layers of Rainforest to shade the white poinsettia petals and Antique Rose to shade the pink poinsettia petals. Apply one to two layers of Blue Spruce to shade all of the holly leaves.

9 PAINT THE VEIN LINES

Using a liner brush and slightly thinned Rainforest, pull the vein lines into the white poinsettia petals and pull the vein lines into the pink poinsettia petals with a mix of Deep Burgundy + a touch of Blue Spruce (1:1). The vein lines of the Mushroom holly leaves are painted with a mix of Mushroom + a touch of Light Ivory, and the Green Mist holly leaf veins are painted with Mushroom.

10 THE SECOND COLOR SHADING

This step will push the vein lines back, which gives added dimension to the petals and leaves. Using the soft-float technique, apply the second shading colors to the poinsettias and holly leaves. Apply the Rainforest to the white poinsettias and Deep Burgundy to the pink poinsettias to shade and separate petals. Apply an additional layer of Blue Spruce to further shade the holly leaves.

11 THIRD COLOR SHADING

Using the soft-float technique again, apply the third shading color, which is a mix of Deep Burgundy + a touch of Blue Spruce (1:1) on the pink poinsettias in the background. Apply the third shading color to the background holly leaves with a mix of Blue Spruce + a touch of Deep Burgundy (1:1). The various levels of shading help distinguish each and every petal and leaf.

12 PAINT THE HIGHLIGHTS

Using a large flat brush corner-loaded with the appropriate color, side-load float along some of the outside edges. On the background white poinsettia petals, highlight the edges with a side-load float of Light Ivory. On the white poinsettia petals in the foreground, highlight the petal edges with a side-load float of White. Highlight the background pink poinsettia petals on the edges with a side-load float of Indiana Rose. On the foreground pink poinsettia petals, highlight the edges with a side-load float of Pink Chiffon. Highlight on the tips of the holly leaves with a side-load float of Ocean Mist Blue.

13 TINTS ON PINK POINSETTIA AND HOLLY LEAVES

Using a large flat brush side-loaded sparingly with Antique Rose, tint some of the white poinsettia petals' edges. Tint the outside edges of several holly leaves with a soft side-load float of Deep Burgundy.

14 PAINT THE VINES, LOOSE LEAF OUTLINES AND SHADOW LEAVES

Using a liner brush loaded with thinned Sable Brown, pull nervous vine lines to attach the holly leaves and berries to the poinsettia petals. Let the vines trail loosely from the design in several additional areas. Using a no. 8 flat brush loaded with thinned Mushroom, paint sheer one-stroke leaves sparing along the vine. Using a liner brush loaded with thinned Rainforest, loosely outline one side of each holly leaf.

Painting Blooms and Blossoms

PAINT THE POINSETTIA CENTERS

15 BASECOAT THE CENTER
Using a no. 3 round brush, opaquely basecoat in the flower center, circles with Hauser Medium Green.

16 SHADE THE CENTER
Using a no. 4 flat brush corner-loaded with Blue Spuce, shade half of each flower center, which is closest to the center point of the flower.

17 PAINT THE RED DOT HIGHLIGHT
Using a stylus, paint a dot of Opaque Red on the highlight half of each flower center.

18 PAINT THE HIGHLIGHT SQUIGGLES
Using a liner brush loaded with Olive Green, make a squiggle line loosely around the red dot highlight in each flower center.

PAINT THE BERRIES

19 BASECOAT THE BERRIES
Using a no. 3 round brush, opaquely basecoat the berries with Indiana Rose.

20 SHADE THE BERRIES
Now is a good time to check and make sure that all of your berries are connected to the design by vines. Using a no. 8 flat brush corner-loaded with Deep Burgundy, shade the half of the berry attached to the vine. Reinforce the berries shaded area with more shading using a mix of Deep Burgundy + a touch of Blue Spruce (1:1).

21 HIGHLIGHT THE BERRIES
Using the tip of the liner brush, paint a small dash or dot on the highlight half of each berry with Light Ivory. Now is the time to use a liner brush loaded with Blue Spruce to clean up any fuzzy edges around the design.

22 FLY-SPECKING
Using an old toothbrush and thinned Light Ivory, fly-speck the inside of the bowl. Load the toothbrush fully with paint, then tap the bristles on a dry paper towel to remove excess moisture. Pull your finger over the bristles to release the paint. You can practice fly-specking on a spare piece of paper or palette pad before you fly-speck directly on your bowl.

Painting Blooms and Blossoms

23 FINISH THE BOWL

Let the bowl dry completely. Brush two to three layers of your favorite acrylic varnish over the inside and outside of the poinsetta bowl. Let the varnish cure for twenty-four hours between layers. Sand lightly between layers with very fine sandpaper or a sanding pad.

TULIPS AND LILACS SCALLOPED BOX

Faux finishes have become popular in all aspects of decorative painting, including walls, furniture and accessory pieces. We thought this beautiful scalloped-top oval box would look nice with an easy faux finish. Any design we add to the base would only enhance the box. We hope you enjoy this design of tulips and lilacs and the finishing treatment on the lid with the coordinating colors.

Paints: D = Delta Ceramcoat; DA = DecoArt Americana; A = Accent

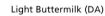

White (D)   Light Buttermilk (DA)   Buttermilk (DA)   Yellow Ochre (DA)

Antique Rose (D)   Taupe (DA)   Violet Haze (D)   Eggplant (A)

Black Plum (DA)   Blue Wisp (D)   Blue Mist (DA)   Jade Green (DA)

Forest Green (D)   Blue Spruce (D)   Hauser Dark Green (DA)   Cool Neutral (DA)

Mix—Forest Green + Blue Wisp + a touch of Blue Spruce   Mix—Hauser Dark Green + Blue Spruce (1:1)   Mix—Violet Haze + a touch of Forest Green mix   Mix—Violet Haze + Buttermilk (1:1)   Mix—Taupe + Light Buttermilk (1:1)

Materials Needed

Brushes
nos. 2, 4, 6, 8, 10, 12 flat
nos. 1, 6/0 liner
Deerfoot stippler
Mop brush

Wood Source
Woodcrafts
(800) 733-4820

Additional Supplies
Stylus
Round sponge
Extender

This pattern may be hand-traced or photo-copied for personal use only. Enlarge at 163 percent to bring it to full size.

Painting Blooms and Blossoms

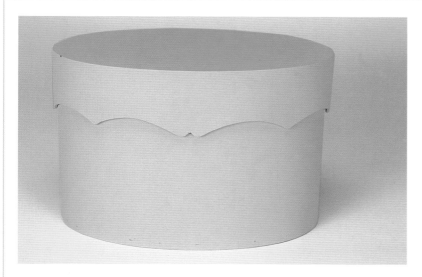

1 BASECOAT THE BOX
Basecoat the entire box with a mix of Taupe + Light Buttermilk + Cool Neutral (1:1:1).

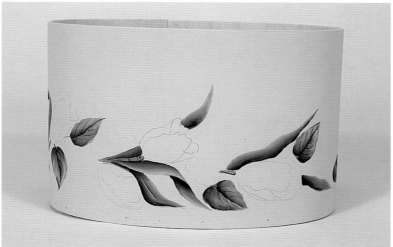

2 PAINT THE LEAVES
Basecoat the leaves with a brush mix of Forest Green, Blue Wisp and Blue Spruce. Mix these colors as you paint the leaves so there is variation in the leaf colors. Shade the leaves with Hauser Dark Green, Blue Spruce or a combination of these two colors. Again it helps to use a variety of leaf colors. Highlight the leaves with a mix of Jade Green + Buttermilk (1:1) or a mix of Blue Mist + Buttermilk (1:1)

THE LEAVES, STEP BY STEP

3 PAINT THE LILACS

Using a small deerfoot stippler brush, lightly stipple the area of the lilac with Violet Haze plus a touch of the basecoat green of the leaves. Double-load a no. 4 flat brush with this stipple color and Eggplant. With the dark to the outside of the petal, make C-strokes to create the lilac blossoms. Paint the dark petals mainly on the bottom with a few petals to the outer top edge.

Make a light lilac mixture of Violet Haze + Buttermilk (3:1). To create the second layer of petals, double-load your flat brush with the light lilac mix and the stipple color. Paint the third layer of petals with a double load of the light lilac mix and Buttermilk. Paint the fourth petal layer with a double load of the light lilac mix plus White.

Paint the lilac centers with Yellow Ochre dots made with your stylus. Add some dark dots around the bottom edge of the center and some White dots toward the top of the center for highlight.

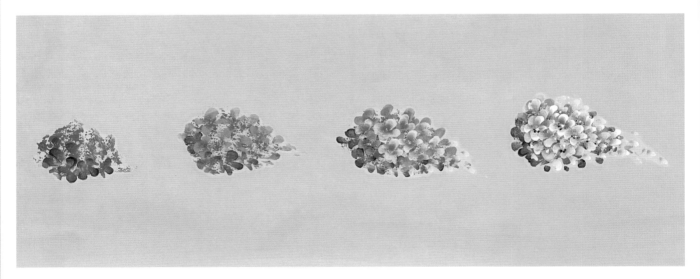

LILACS, STEP BY STEP

Painting Blooms and Blossoms

PAINT THE TULIPS

4 SOFT-FLOAT TECHNIQUE, STEP 1
Basecoat the tulips with one layer of Buttermilk. Let this dry completely. Moisten the tulip with clean water. Using a large flat brush corner-loaded with Antique Rose, apply the first layer of shading on the tulips.

5 SOFT-FLOAT TECHNIQUE, STEP 2
Remember to let the paint dry completely between steps, and moisten the tulip with clean water before each shading. Deepen the shading using a large flat brush corner-loaded with Black Plum. Pit-pat the color onto the damp surface.

6 SOFT-FLOAT TECHNIQUE, STEP 3

Immediately after applying the shading color on the damp surface, stipple softly over the color with a dry mop brush. Wipe the brush often on a clean paper towel or terry towel to keep it dry. Do not wash the brush until you have finished your painting session for the day.

❧ **HINT** ❧ *The dry mop brush stippling softens the shading color and removes any brush strokes.*

7 SHADING LINES, HIGHLIGHTS, FINAL SHADING AND TINTS

Using a liner brush loaded with thinned Black Plum, pull shading lines from the tulip bases. Using a large flat brush corner-loaded heavily with White, highlight the top edge of the tulip petals. Deepen the V areas of the tulips with a side-load float of Eggplant. Using a large flat brush corner-loaded sparingly with Yellow Ochre or Eggplant, tint the edges of some of the tulip petals.

THE TULIPS, STEP BY STEP

8 TINT THE LEAVES; PAINT THE VEIN LINES AND TENDRILS

Using a liner brush loaded with a thinned mix of Hauser Dark Green + a touch of Black Plum, attach the leaves to the tulips and lilacs. Using the same mix, pull vein lines into the heart-shaped leaves and pull loose tendrils from the main design. These elements will loosen the overall look of the design. Using a large flat brush corner-loaded with Black Plum or Egg-plant, tint the outside edges of a few heart-shaped leaves.

❧ **Faux Finishing the Lid** ❧

1. Dampen the surface.

2. Apply the color.

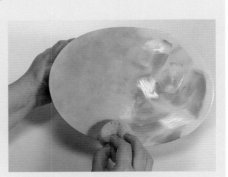

3. Blend the color

Painting Blooms and Blossoms

9 FINISH THE BOX

Let the box dry completely. Brush two to three layers of your favorite acrylic varnish over the inside and outside of the tulip and lilac box. Let the varnish cure for twenty-four hours between layers. Sand lightly between layers with very fine sandpaper or a sanding pad.

FRUIT SAMPLER

This project includes four small fruits: cherries, raspberries, blueberries and grapes. By having a separate design for each fruit, you can concentrate on one fruit at a time. These designs may be grouped together on the four-drawer box shown at left, or you can paint each one individually on other surfaces, such as a small box or coffee mug.

Paint: D = Delta Ceramcoat; DA = DecoArt Americana; A = Accent

White (D)

Light Buttermilk (DA)

Buttermilk (DA)

Yellow Ochre (DA)

Sable Brown (DA)

Driftwood (DA)

Charcoal Grey (DA)

Raw Umber (A)

Rose Cloud (D)

Lisa Pink (D)

Pink Parfait (D)

Dusty Mauve (D)

Sweetheart Blush (D)

Black Cherry (D)

Black Plum (DA)

Pansy Lavender (DA)

Vintage Wine (D)

Aquamarine (D)

Liberty Blue (D)

Midnight Blue (D)

Mushroom (A)

Shale Green (DA)

Dark Forest Green (D)

Blue Spruce (D)

Black (D)

Mix—Sweetheart Blush + Midnight Blue (1:1)

Mix—Midnight Blue + Black Cherry (1:1)

Mix—Vintage Wine + Pansy Lavender (1:1)

Mix—Vintage Wine + Pansy Lavender + White (1:1:1)

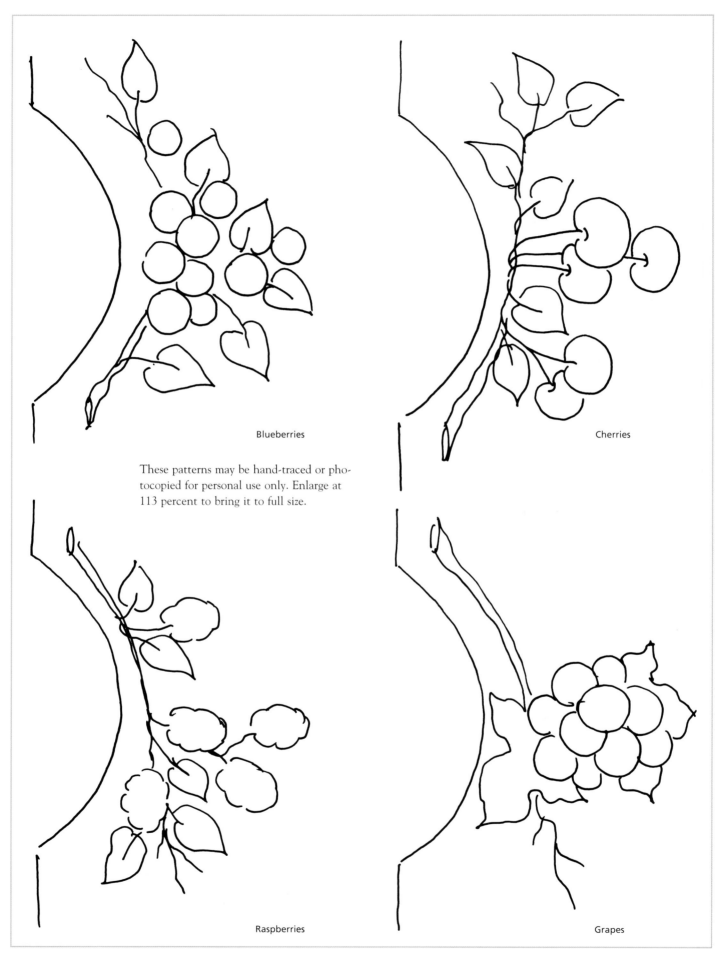

Blueberries

These patterns may be hand-traced or photocopied for personal use only. Enlarge at 113 percent to bring it to full size.

Cherries

Raspberries

Grapes

Painting Blooms and Blossoms

Brushes
nos. 6/0, 1 liner
nos. 2, 4, 6, 8, 10, 12 flats
nos. 1, 3 round
Minimop

Wood Source
Four-drawer recipe box
Wayne's Woodenware

Additional Supplies
Winsor & Newton Burnt Umber oil
    paint
Odorless turpentine
Old rags
Minwax Ipswich Pine Stain
¾"-wide (1.9cm) transparent tape

1 SURFACE PREPARATION

Stain the entire box with Minwax Ipswich Pine Stain. Basecoat the drawer fronts with Blue Spruce.

2 BASECOAT THE BRANCHES

Using a no. 3 round brush, basecoat the branches with a mix of Charcoal Grey + Raw Umber (1:1).

3 OVERSTROKE THE BRANCHES

Overstroke the branches using a no. 10 flat brush loaded with Driftwood. You can brush mix Driftwood and Light Buttermilk for some color variety. Complete the branches with thin wiggle lines of Charcoal Grey.

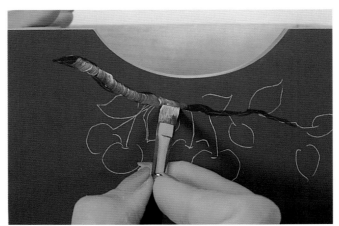

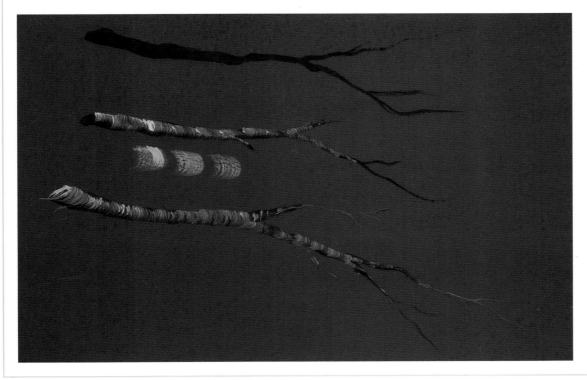

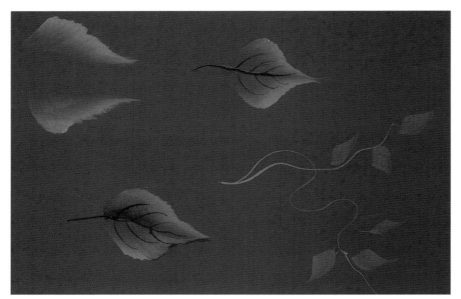

4 PAINT THE LEAVES

Using a no. 8 flat brush double-loaded with Dark Forest Green and Mushroom or Dark Forest Green and Shale Green, paint the main leaves with the one-stroke leaf technique. Paint the leaf veins with Raw Umber. Using a no. 6 flat brush, paint the filler leaves with one strokes of a Sable Brown + Mushroom mix (1:1). The tendrils are painted with Sable Brown.

5 PAINT THE BLUEBERRIES

Basecoat the blueberries with Liberty Blue using a no. 6 flat brush. Shade the blueberry's stem end with a float of Midnight Blue using a no. 8 flat brush. Also with a no. 8 flat brush, highlight the opposite side of the berry with a float of Aquamarine. Create the blossom end with crisscross lines of Black using a 6/0 liner brush.

Highlight the blossom end with a wiggly float of Aquamarine + White (1:1) using a no. 4 flat brush. Add a dash of White to create a highlight shine. Using a no. 8 flat brush, tint some of the berries in the shade area with a float of Midnight Blue + Black Cherry (1:1). Tint some of the main leaves with Black Cherry or with one of the berry colors.

THE BLUEBERRIES, STEP BY STEP

Painting Blooms and Blossoms

6 PAINT THE RASPBERRIES

Basecoat the raspberries with Sweetheart Blush using a no. 6 flat brush. Using a no. 4 flat brush, shade the raspberries with dark C-strokes of a Sweetheart Blush + Midnight Blue mix (1:1). Highlight the raspberries with light C-strokes using a no. 4 flat brush loaded with a mix of Sweetheart Blush + White (3:1).

Outline all the C-strokes with the highlight mix and a touch more White using a 6/0 liner brush. Using a no. 8 flat brush, float over the shade side of the berry with a soft float of Vintage Wine. Then, use a no. 4 flat brush to highlight some of the light C-strokes with a float of Rose Cloud. Add a dot of White for the highlight shine. Create the calyxes with small one strokes of Dark Forest Green using a no. 1 round brush. Tint some of the main leaves with Sweetheart Blush or Vintage Wine using a no. 8 flat brush.

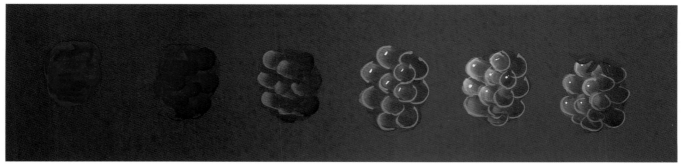

THE RASPBERRIES, STEP BY STEP

7 PAINT THE CHERRIES

Using a no. 8 flat brush, basecoat the cherries with Dusty Mauve. Shade one side of the cherries with a float of Black Cherry using a no. 8 flat brush. Allow the cherries to dry completely. Wet them with clean water and dab a dot of Pink Parfait in the highlight area, mopping it out with a minimop brush. Repeat the highlight area with Lisa Pink. Add a dash of White in the highlight area for shine. Paint the stem depression at the top of the cherry with a C-stroke of Black Cherry and a touch of Dark Forest Green. Paint the cherry stems with Sable Brown plus a touch of Raw Umber. To separate the cherries, use a no. 10 flat brush and a float of Black Plum. Tint the main leaves with a float of Dusty Mauve or Black Cherry.

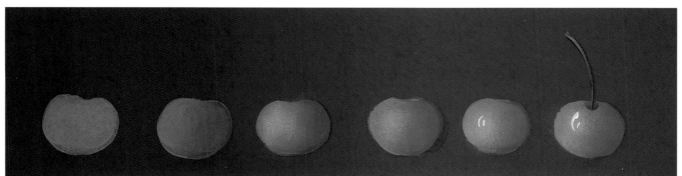

THE CHERRIES, STEP BY STEP

8 PAINT THE GRAPES

Basecoat the darkest grapes using a no. 6 flat brush loaded with Vintage Wine. Lightly highlight the outer edge of the dark grapes with a float of Vintage Wine + Pansy Lavender (2:1). Basecoat the midvalue grapes with Vintage Wine + Pansy Lavender (1:1). Highlight these grapes with the basecoat mix plus a touch of White. Basecoat the lightest grapes with the highlight mix of the midvalue grapes. Highlight these grapes with more White added to the mix. Shade these grapes with the Vintage Wine + Pansy Lavender mix (1:1). On the lighter grapes, add a dash of White for shine. Tint the main leaves with Vintage Wine or Black Cherry.

THE GRAPES, STEP BY STEP

9 PAINT THE BLOSSOMS

Double-load a no. 6 flat brush with Mushroom and Buttermilk. With the Buttermilk to the outside of the petal, stand on the chisel edge of the brush, press down and return to the chisel edge of the brush to create a petal. Paint the blossom centers with Yellow Ochre and shade with Black Cherry.

Painting Blooms and Blossoms

The Blueberry Blossoms

The Raspberry Blossoms

The Cherry Blossoms

The Grape Blossoms

10 FINISHING THE BOX

Tape the two sides and front edge of the top with ¾″-wide (1.9 cm) transparent tape. Leave a space of ½″ (1.3cm) and tape again. Paint this ½″ (1.3cm) space with Blue Spruce. Antique the edges of the outer box with Burnt Umber oil paint. Allow the antiquing to dry completely and erase any visible graphite lines. Finally, apply three coats of acrylic varnish.

FRUIT RECIPE BOX

P ainting fruit has never been easier, so don't feel intimidated to try these pears, apples and plums. This recipe box will complement the Fruit Sampler very nicely.

Materials Needed

Brushes
nos. 4, 8, 10, ¾-inch (1.9cm), 1-inch (2.54cm)
no. 1, 3 liner
½-inch (1.3cm) rake
Foam brush (optional)

Wood Source
Wayne's Woodenware

Additional Supplies
¾"-wide (1.9cm) transparent tape
Odorless mineral spirits
Clean, soft rags
Cotton swabs
Minwax Ipswich Pine Stain
Winsor & Newton Burnt Umber oil paint
Acrylic varnish

Paints: D = Delta Ceramcoat; DA = DecoArt Americana; A = Accent

White (D)

Buttermilk (DA)

Maple Sugar Tan (D)

Yellow Ochre (DA)

Straw (DA)

Antique Gold (DA)

Sable Brown (DA)

Raw Sienna (DA)

Mocha Brown (D)

Burnt Sienna (DA)

Mushroom (A)

Blue Spruce (D)

Forest Green (D)

Dark Forest Green (DA)

Black Green (D)

Santa Red (DA)

Pink Parfait (D)

Dusty Mauve (D)

Black Cherry (D)

Black Plum (D)

Pansy Lavender (D)

Vintage Wine (D)

Mix—Santa Red + Black Cherry (1:1)

Mix—Raw Sienna + Yellow Ochre (2:1)

This pattern may be hand-traced or photo-copied for personal use only. Enlarge at 120 percent to bring it to full size.

Painting Blooms and Blossoms

SURFACE PREPARATION

1 STAIN THE BOX
Using an old rag or disposable foam brush, varnish the raw wood recipe box with Minwax Ipswich Pine Stain. Let this dry completely, then sand lightly.

Tape the inserts on the lid and base of the recipe box using a quality ¾"-wide (1.9cm) transparent tape. Tape the lid along the outside edge to preserve a ¾"-wide (1.9cm) band of stained wood around the lid. Tape the base of the recipe box over the bottom routed edge to keep it clean. Then press a line of tape 1½" (3.8cm) from the bottom edge of the recipe box. Basecoat these two areas with two layers of Blue Spruce. When the paint is dry, remove the tape.

2 TRANSFER THE PATTERN AND SHADE THE BACKGROUND
Using worn graphite paper and a stylus, transfer your pattern onto the recipe box. Using a large flat brush corner-loaded sparingly with Black Green, softly shade behind the main elements of the design.

⊷ HINT ⊶ *It will be easier to control the softness of the shading if you dampen the surface with clean water before applying the background shading. To keep this shading soft, work one small section at a time.*

3 PAINT THE MAIN LEAVES

Double-load a no. 8 flat brush heavily with Dark Forest Green and Mushroom. Blend these colors well on your palette. Keep the Mushroom edge of the brush to the outside edge of the leaf. Begin the main leaf at the base, painting half of the leaf at a time. To begin the leaf stroke, position the brush at the leaf's base perpendicular to the center vein line. Apply pressure to the brush, flattening the bristles. Slide the brush back and forth to create ripples in the leaves. Move the brush down one side of the leaf, slowly pivoting to the chisel edge of the brush as you slide your way to the tip of the leaf. Repeat for the opposite side, allowing the paint to overlap in the middle of the leaf.

PAINT THE PEARS, PLUMS AND APPLES

4 THE PEARS

Thoroughly basecoat the pear with Antique Gold. Apply the first layer of shading along the bottom, on top and at the indentation of the horizontal pear. Separate the two pears with a wide side-load float of Mocha Brown. Repeat this color shading until the area is wide and rich in value. Reinforce the shaded area with a side-load float of Burnt Sienna. Again, repeat as necessary until the shaded area is wide and rich in value. Further deepen the shaded areas with a side-load float of Burnt Sienna + a touch of Black Cherry mix. Highlight the fullest part of the horizontal pear and the stem end of the vertical pear with a wide side-load float of Straw. Reinforce these areas with an additional highlight of Straw + a touch of White mix. Add just enough White to slightly lighten the Straw. Using a small flat brush, side-load float in the stem hollows with Burnt Sienna. Paint the pear stems using Sable Brown. Deepen the base with a line of Sable Brown + a touch of Black Green. Lightly spatter the pears with thinned Burnt Sienna. I like to protect the rest of the design area with tissue, cutting it to fit around the pears.

❧ **HINT** ❧ *When highlighting the two pears, the foreground curve is highlighted stronger than the background curve.*

5 THE PLUM

Basecoat the plum with Black Cherry. Shade the bottom of the plum and in the crease with a side-load float of Vintage Wine + a touch of Black Green mix. Highlight the two fullest parts of the plum with a side-load float of Pansy Lavender.

Painting Blooms and Blossoms

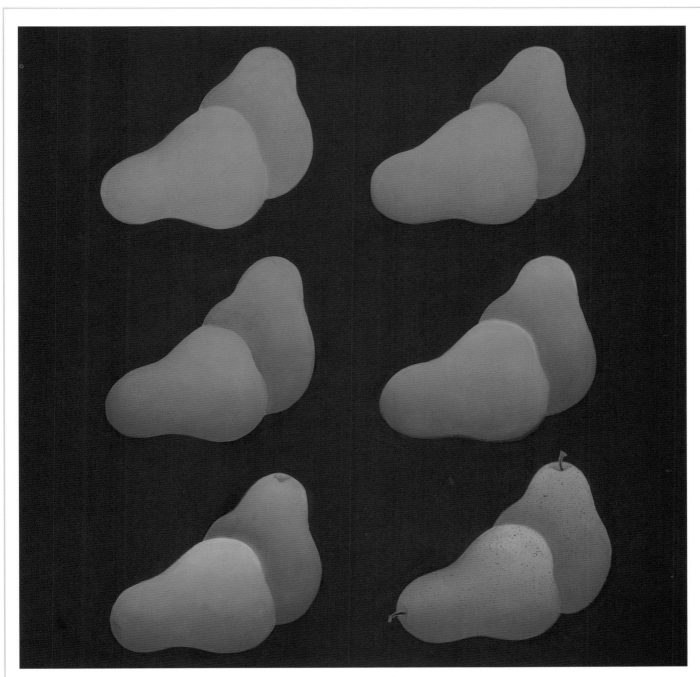

PEAR, STEP BY STEP

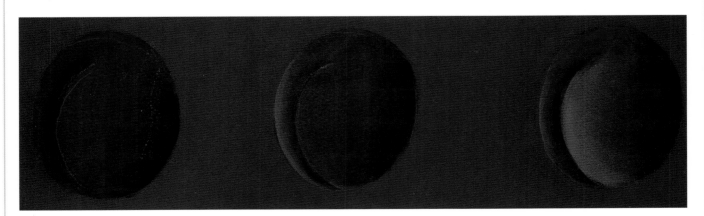

PLUM, STEP BY STEP

6 THE APPLE

Thoroughly basecoat the apple with Maple Sugar Tan. Let this dry completely. Using a ½-inch (1.3cm) rake brush loaded with slightly thinned Santa Red, brush the highlight lines onto the apple's surface. Paint the lines to follow the apple's shape. The soft-float technique works best when painting the apple. Use a dry mop brush to soften the shading layers and to mop out and preserve the highlight area. Be sure to let the apple dry completely between each layer of shading. Using the soft-float technique and a large flat brush corner-loaded with Santa Red, side-load float the outside edges of the apple. Next, shade the stem hollow, top and bottom of the apple with a side-load float of Santa Red. Reinforce the shaded areas with an additional side-load float of Santa Red + a touch of Black Cherry. Deepen the stem hollow, upper left area and lower right area of the apple with a side-load float of Santa Red + Black Cherry (1:1). Repeat this final shading step. Paint the apple stem with Sable Brown deepened at the base with a mix of Sable Brown + a touch of Black Green. When this is completely dry and your apple is too bright for the composition, paint a wash over the entire apple with a sheer layer of Black Plum.

THE APPLE, STEP BY STEP

Painting Blooms and Blossoms

7 PAINT THE LEAF VEINS, VINES AND SHADOW LEAVES

Using a liner brush loaded with thinned Sable Brown, paint veins in the main leaves and pull loose vining on the design. Using a no. 4 flat brush double-loaded with Mushroom and Sable Brown, paint one-stroke filler leaves and a few smaller versions of the main leaves sparingly along the vines.

PAINT THE PURPLE AND GREEN GRAPES AND CHERRIES

8 THE PURPLE GRAPES

Using a no. 8 flat brush, basecoat the purple grapes with Vintage Wine. On the background purple grapes, highlight half of each grape with a side-load float of Pansy Lavender. On the foreground purple grapes, shade one side of each grape with Vintage Wine, highlight the opposite half of each grape with a side-load float of Vintage Wine + (a mix of Pansy Lavender + a touch of White).

9 THE GREEN GRAPES

Basecoat the green grapes with Forest Green using the no. 8 flat brush. On the background green grapes, highlight half of each grape with a side-load float of Mushroom. On the foreground grapes, shade one side of each grape with a side-load float of Forest Green. Highlight the opposite half of each grape with a side-load float of Forest Green + (Mushroom + a touch of White).

10 THE CHERRIES

Basecoat the cherries with Dusty Mauve. Shade the left side of each cherry with a side-load float of Black Cherry, and highlight the opposite half of each cherry with a side-load float of Pink Parfait. Paint a small stem hollow with a line of Black Green. Paint the cherry stem with Sable Brown, shaded at the base with a line of Black Green.

11 TINT THE MAIN LEAVES AND GRAPES

Using a large flat brush, tint a few edges and centers of the main leaves with a light side-load float of Black Cherry. Tint a few of the background purple grapes by washing over the individual grape with a light wash of Black Cherry. Tint some background green grapes by washing over the individual grape with sheer Sable Brown.

12 SHADE THE MAIN LEAVES AND GREEN GRAPES

Using a large flat brush corner-loaded sparingly with Black Green, side-load float between the main leaves where they overlap. This will separate and push some of the leaves to the back. On the green grapes, side-load float Black Green in the shade areas as needed to define shapes.

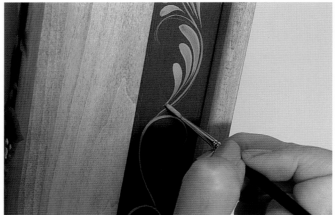

13 PAINT THE FILLER FLOWERS AND FINAL HIGHLIGHTING

Using a no. 4 flat brush corner-loaded heavily with Buttermilk, paint small C-strokes to form filler flower clusters. Position these clusters to fill holes in the design. Using a small stipple brush double-loaded and overblended with Yellow Ochre and Black Cherry, tap small centers into the filler flower clusters. Using a liner brush loaded with Light Ivory, paint a small comma stroke in the highlight area of each purple grape, green grape and cherry.

❧ HINT ❧ *Notice how the grapes in the foreground receive the stronger highlight stroke. The background grapes receive just a dash of highlight.*

14 PAINT THE STROKEWORK BORDER

Using a liner brush loaded with a mix of Raw Sienna + Yellow Ochre (2:1), paint the thin curved lines (spine) of the border.

❧ HINT ❧ *Position your hand so you are pulling the brush into the curves instead of pushing the brush ahead of your hand. This will give you more control over your brush.*

Using a no. 3 round brush, paint the comma strokes along the spine of the strokework border. Load your brush fully with paint and start with the brush at the head of the stroke, allowing the bristles to spread before you. Slowly pull and lift the brush to form the tail.

STROKEWORK BORDER, STEP BY STEP

15 STRIPING, VARNISHING AND ANTIQUING
Using a liner brush loaded with Blue Spruce, paint a line along the top back edge of the recipe box lid, following the curve of the box. To antique, brush on one layer of acrylic varnish. Let cure twenty-four hours. Using a soft rag, moisten the areas to be antiqued with odorless mineral spirits. Rub a generous amount of Burnt Umber oil paint along the edges of the box, softening with a clean rag. Remove any antiquing from the highlight areas in the design with a clean rag or cotton swabs. Let this dry completely. Brush on two to three more layers of acrylic varnish. Let the varnish cure twenty-four hours and sand lightly between the layers.

FLORAL SAMPLER FLOORCLOTH

Now you can combine all the new floral techniques you've learned in this book for a beautiful floorcloth! Paint this combination project to beautify your garden room, kitchen or bath. Floorcloths are very durable and the surface is wonderful to paint on. The texture of the preprimed floorcloth makes shading and floating color a breeze.

This pattern may be hand-traced or photocopied for personal use only. Enlarge at 188 percent to bring it to full size.

Materials Needed

Brushes
nos. 4, 8, 12, ¾-inch (1.9cm), 1-inch (2.54cm) flat
no. 1 liner
no. 4 script liner
no. 3 round
¾-inch (1.9cm) rake
Foam roller

Source
Preprimed 2′ × 3′ (61cm × 91.4cm) floorcloth from Hollins Enterprises, Inc.

Additional Supplies
Small round sponge
T-square
Chalk pencil
Quality masking tape
Acrylic varnish

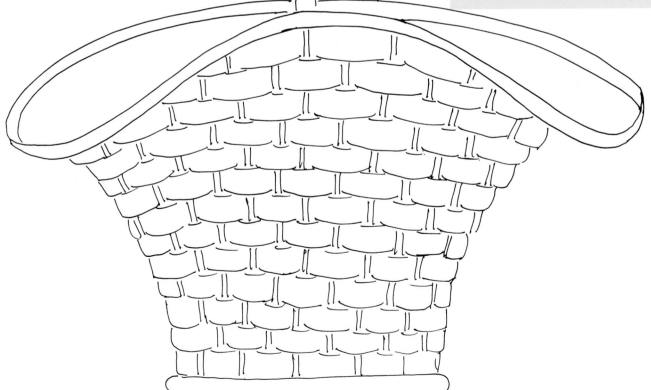

This pattern may be hand-traced or photo-copied for personal use only. Enlarge at 176 percent to bring it to full size.

Buttermilk (DA) · Shale Green (DA) · White (D) · Light Buttermilk (DA) · Desert Sand (DA) · Taffy Cream (DA)

Yellow Ochre (DA) · Pale Yellow (D) · Crocus Yellow (D) · Cadmium Yellow (DA) · Golden Straw (DA) · Antique Gold (D)

Golden Brown (D) · Spice Tan (D) · Raw Sienna (D) · Raw Sienna (DA) · Burnt Sienna (DA) · Burnt Umber (D)

Raw Umber (D) · Lilac Dusk (D) · Wisteria (D) · Violet Haze (DA) · Pansy Lavender (DA) · Vintage Wine (D)

Dioxazine Purple (DA) · Eggplant (A) · Black Plum (DA) · Rose Petal Pink (D) · Antique Rose (D) · Pink Parfait (D)

Wild Rose (D) · Raspberry (DA) · French Mocha (DA) · Dusty Mauve (D) · Deep Burgundy (DA) · Black Cherry (D)

Blue Wisp (D) · Blue Mist (DA) · Olive Green (DA) · Jade Green (DA) · Wedgewood Green (D)

Forest Green (D) · Hauser Dark Green (DA) · Blue Spruce (D) · Payne's Grey (D) · Hauser Medium Green (DA)

1 PREPARE THE FLOORCLOTH

Purchase a preprimed floorcloth measuring 2′ × 3′ (61cm × 91.4cm). The one available from Hollins Enterprises Inc. is primed on the front and back. It's ready to paint! Preprimed canvas is available in many sizes so you can customize the size of your floorcloth, or you can cut table runners and placemats to complement your floorcloth. Basecoat one side of the floorcloth with Buttermilk. It is easy to basecoat canvas by rolling the paint on with a small foam roller. Let this dry completely. Mark off the outside border area with a pencil line 3″ (7.6cm) from the perimeter of the floorcloth. Spatter the floorcloth with thinned Spice Brown with extra heavy spattering in the four corners before the border area. Transfer the main pattern lines using worn graphite and your stylus.

PAINT THE BASKET

2 BASECOAT THE BASKET

Basecoat the basket with a sheer layer of Raw Sienna. Don't worry about a smooth coat. This color serves as a background color only.

3 PAINT THE BASKET SLATS

Using a no. 4 flat brush loaded with Spice Tan, paint short vertical lines to indicate the spokes of the basket. Using a no. 12 or larger flat brush loaded with slightly thinned Raw Sienna, paint horizontal slats or the weavers on the basket. Let a little of the background color show through between the weavers. Curve the weavers slightly to resemble a handwoven basket

4 SHADE THE BASKET, STEP 1

Using a large flat brush side-loaded with Spice Brown, shade the left side of each horizontal basket weaver.

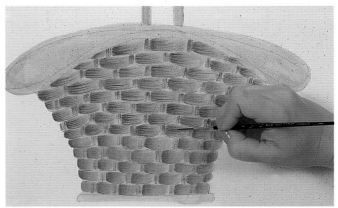

5 PAINT THE SHADING LINES

Using a liner brush loaded with slightly thinned Spice Brown, paint shading lines on top of the horizontal weaver's shaded area. Using the liner brush loaded with Spice Brown, paint a few shading lines coming down from the top of each vertical spoke.

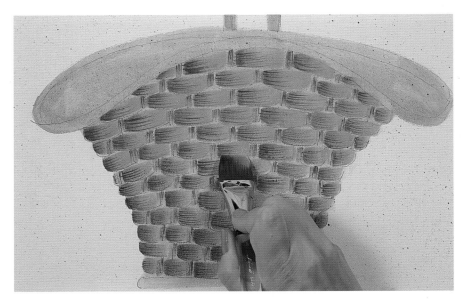

6 HIGHLIGHT THE BASKET
Using a large flat brush side-loaded with Antique Gold, float a highlight on the right side of each horizontal weaver. No highlight is needed on the vertical spokes.

7 PAINT THE BASKET RIM AND HANDLE
Using a no. 8 flat heavily double-loaded with Spice Brown and Antique Gold, paint the S-stroke border for the basket handle, top and bottom of the basket rim. To paint the S-stroke, start on the chisel edge of your brush. Apply slight pressure as you slide the brush forward and down releasing pressure. Return to the chisel edge.

8 SHADE THE BASKET, STEP 2
Using a large flat brush corner-loaded with a mix of Burnt Sienna + Raw Umber (2:1), side-load float shading under the basket rim, down the left side, across the bottom above the rim, inside the curved opening and on the handle where it tucks into the basket. Try the soft-float technique to achieve wide, soft shading. It will take two to three layers to get the proper value depth in the shaded areas.

Painting Blooms and Blossoms

9 SPONGE THE BACKGROUND FOLIAGE

With a small round sponge, lightly sponge in the background behind the flowers with Forest Green.

10 PAINT THE LEAVES

Basecoat the leaves with a mix of Forest Green and Blue Wisp. Brush mix these colors as you go so they are not all the same. Shade the leaves with Hauser Dark Green, Blue Spruce or any combination of these two colors. Highlight the leaves with Jade Green, Blue Mist and either of these colors mixed with Buttermilk. See the Tulips and Lilacs Scalloped Box project on page 81 for more information.

11 THE LILACS
Sponge in the lilac areas lightly with a mix of Violet Haze and a touch of the leaf basecoat mix. Use the same mixture with Eggplant added for the darkest petals. Paint the second petals with a double load of this mixture with a mix of Violet Haze + Buttermilk (3:1). Paint the third layer of petals with a double load of the lighter mixture plus Buttermilk. Paint the top layer of petals with a double load of the lighter mixture and White. Paint the centers with dots of Yellow Ochre, with a few dark mix dots for shade and one White dot for highlight. The step-by-step photos are in the Tulips and Lilacs Scalloped Box project on page 82.

12 THE ASTERS
Paint the aster petals with a no. 3 round brush as one-stroke layers. Paint the first layer of stroke petals with a mix of Deep Burgundy + a touch of Black Plum. Paint the second layer of stroke petals with Raspberry. Paint the third layer of stroke petals with a mix of Raspberry + a touch of White. Add just enough White to see a value change. Paint the fourth layer of stroke petals with a mix of the previous Raspberry/White combination + more White. On the fourth layer of stroke petals, brush mix in the White so you have a variety of petal colors. Paint the fourth layer of stroke petals within the highlight section of the aster. Paint the partial asters as layers of one strokes using the first, second and third layers of aster colors. Using a no. 4 flat brush double-loaded with English Yew and Black Green, paint calyxes on the partial asters as three small one-stroke leaves. Basecoat the centers with a stipple of Golden Brown and shade with a Burnt Sienna stipple. Use a stipple of Taffy Cream as the highlight color. Paint very small dots of Black Plum around the shaded half of the flower center and very small dots of Taffy Cream around the highlight half of the flower center.

13 THE TULIPS

Basecoat the tulips with one semisheer layer of Buttermilk. Separate each tulip petal with a soft float of Antique Rose. Repeat to deepen the shade areas if needed. Deepen some of the previously shaded areas with a soft float of sheer Black Plum. Using a liner brush loaded with thinned Black Plum, pull thin shading lines from the base of the tulips. Using a large flat brush heavily corner-loaded with White, highlight the top edges of the tulip petals. Reinforce the darkest shading with a side-load float of sheer Eggplant. Tint the edges of some tulip petals with a sheer side-load float of Yellow Ochre.

14 THE PANSIES

Basecoat the pink pansy petals with a sheer layer of Antique Rose. Using a soft float of Black Cherry, shade one to two times for added depth. Highlight the outside edges of the pink petals with a side-load float of Pink Parfait. Basecoat the white petals with Antique White. Shade these petals one to two times using a soft float of Honey Brown. Pull Vintage Wine shading lines onto the white petals. Highlight the outside edges of the white petals with a side-load float of White. Basecoat the yellow petals with a sheer layer of Yellow Ochre. Shade these petals one to two times using a soft float of Honey Brown. Pull Vintage Wine shading lines onto the yellow petals. Highlight the outside edges of the yellow petals with a side-load float of Pale Yellow. Paint the flower centers as two small strokes of Pale Yellow.

PAINT THE FILLER FLOWERS

15 THE APPLE BLOSSOMS
Basecoat the apple blossom petals with Buttermilk. Shade the petals with a double load of Buttermilk plus a mix of Wild Rose + Rose Petal Pink (1:1). Highlight the petals with White. The step by steps are shown in the Apple Blossom Time project on page 54.

16 THE CHAMOMILE FLOWERS
Paint the stems and leaves with Forest Green using a fine liner brush. Create the flowers with small strokes of White. Paint the center with Golden Straw and Spice Brown for shading. This flower step-by-step is shown in the Flowering Herb Plate on page 42.

17 THE EVENING PRIMROSE FLOWERS
Paint the stems with Wedgewood Green. Using a no. 8 flat brush, paint the leaves with a double-loaded one stroke of Forest Green into Wedgewood Green. Paint the flowers with a double-loaded C-stroke of White and Golden Straw. The yellow goes to the outside of the panel. The center is a brush mix of Golden Straw plus a touch of Spice Brown. Paint the stamen with the center mix plus a touch more Spice Brown. This flower is shown step by step in the Flowering Herb Plate project on page 44.

Painting Blooms and Blossoms

18 THE LAVENDER FLOWERS
Paint the stems with Wedgewood Green. Brush mix Wedgewood Green and Shale Green for the leaves. Paint the flowers with very small C-strokes of Pansy Lavender, Dioxazine Purple and White. This flower is shown step by step in the Flowering Herb Plate project on page 41.

19 THE THYME FLOWERS
Paint the stems and leaves with a thin mix of Forest Green + Wedgewood Green (1:1). Paint the veins with Forest Green. Brush mix French Mauve and Antique Rose with an occasional touch of White for the flowers. These flowers are shown step by step in the Flowering Herb Plate project on page 45.

20 PAINT THE VINES AND SHADOW LEAVES
Fill in any open areas with some loose vines painted with Spice Brown. Paint the shadow leaves along the vine with very thin stroke leaves of Shale Green.

PAINT THE BORDER

21 BASECOAT AND MARK OFF THE BORDER

Basecoat the 3″ (7.6cm) border with Shale Green. Let this dry completely. Using a chalk pencil and T-square, mark the main rake stripe lines 1½″ (3.8cm) apart. Start marking vertically ¾″ (1.9cm) from the inside edge of the border on both sides. Continue with the vertical lines on the top and bottom borders, spacing them 1½″ (3.8cm) apart, fudging a little in the middle of the top and bottom if necessary. Repeat the process horizontally by marking the first lines ¾″ (1.9cm) from the top and bottom edges of the border. Continue with the horizontal lines on the sides of the floorcloth border, spacing them 1½″ (3.8cm) apart, fudging just a little in the middle if necessary. Using a ¾″ (1.9cm) rake brush loaded with slighly thinned Desert Sand, paint a stripe on top of each horizontal and vertical line, keeping the chalk line in the middle of the stripe.

22 PAINT THE PINK LINE

Using a long script liner and slightly thinned Antique Rose, paint a line ⅛″ (0.3cm) from the top edge of each horizontal rake stripe.

✺ HINT ✺ You might find it easier to paint long lines if you look slightly ahead of your brush and pull toward yourself, balancing your hand with your pinky finger.

23 PAINT THE PURPLE LINE
Using a long script liner loaded with slighly thinned Wisteria, paint a line ⅛" (0.3cm) to the left of each vertical purple line. Next, paint a line ⅛" (0.3cm) below each horizontal purple line.

24 PAINT THE WHITE LINE
Using a long script liner loaded with slightly thinned Buttermilk, paint a line ⅛" (0.3cm) to the left of each vertical purple line. Next, paint a line ⅛" (0.3cm) below each horizontal purple line.

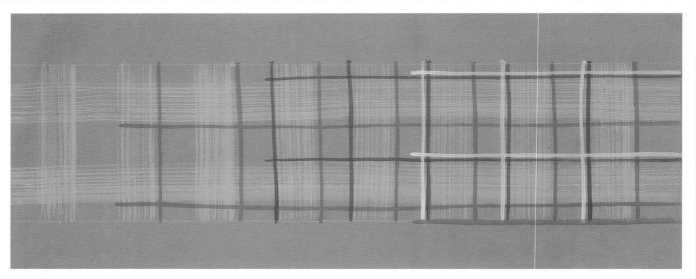

PAINTING THE BORDER, STEP BY STEP

FINISH THE FLOORCLOTH

25 THE FLOORCLOTH BORDER
Using a long script liner loaded with a slightly thinned mix of Antique Rose + Mushroom (4:1), paint a line around the perimeter of the painted center next to the border. This line will cover any fuzzy edges between the floorcloth center and the border.

🎗 **Caring for Your Floorcloth** 🎗
To keep the floorcloth from slipping on the floor, glue on strips of Rubbermaid webbing—used to line drawers—or brush on swatches of rubber cement. Once a year or as you notice the varnish loosing its shine, wash the floorcloth with soapy water and dry completely. Then apply one to two new layers of acrylic varnish.

26 VARNISH THE FLOORCLOTH

Brush on two to three layers of your favorite acrylic varnish. Varnish the front and back of the floorcloth. Alternate varnishing between the front and back of the floorcloth so it will not curl on the edges. Let the varnish cure twenty-four hours between each layer.

Gallery

Now that you know how to paint
blooms and blossoms, here are a few
more ideas!

FRUIT BOX

FRUIT BOX LID

POINSETTIA BOX

POINSETTIA BOX LID

THYME PLATE

TARRAGON PLATE

ROSEMARY PLATE

LAVENDER PLATE

Painting Blooms and Blossoms

FRUIT AND BERRY BOWL

Terms and Techniques

C-Stroke A side-load application of color. Starting on the chisel of the brush, apply pressure to draw the letter C, releasing pressure to return to the chisel edge and complete the "letter."

Comma/One Stroke Load the brush generously with paint. Apply pressure at the head of the stroke and release pressure to paint the tail of the stroke.

Dashes Used in corners of designs or to break up a length of striping. Using the tip of the liner brush, touch the surface to paint each dash.

Double Load To double-load a brush, dip one corner of a lightly dampened brush into paint color no. 1, covering about half of the width of the brush. Next, dip the opposite corner of the brush into paint color no. 2. Stroke the loaded brush on waxed palette until you have a soft blend of color from one corner of the brush to the other. Make sure to blend both sides of the brush.

Flip-Flop Float Load the brush as in a side-load float, with the concentration of color on one side of the flat brush blending to clear water on the other side of brush. Apply the color edge of the brush along the center of the area to be highlighted, then flip your brush over, applying color on the other side of the highlighted center, overlapping and softening where the color meets. Keep the color edge of the paintbrush to the center of the highlight area, and keep the water edge of the paintbrush to the outside edges of the highlight area and then flip the brush and repeat on the opposite side. Let dry, building two to three layers to achieve a strong highlight.

Highlighting and Shading When the directions call for shading, paint with a color darker than the basecoat. When the directions call for highlighting, paint with a color lighter than the basecoat.

Linework Thin your paint with water to an ink-like consistency. Load the brush fully with paint. Using your pinkie or wrist as a steadying brace, stay on the tip of the liner and pull the linework toward you. A light touch results in a thin line, a heavier touch results in a thicker line.

❧ H I N T ❧ Look just beyond the tip of the brush where you want the line to go, rather than at the tip of the brush. This helps you to paint a straighter line.

Mop Technique for Shading or Highlighting Solidly basecoat in the appropriate color. This may take two or three coats to get a nice even coverage. The basecoat must be completely dry before you can do any shading or highlighting. I have at least two mops ready, one for shading and one for highlighting. (You cannot wash out a mop and use it when it is wet.) When the basecoat is dry, re-wet the entire surface with a wet water wash of the base color (thin the base color in a lot of water) or with clean water. Side-load into your shade color and apply into one area of shading. Mop out the shadow softly. Let the surface dry each time. You may have to repeat this step several times to get the shade color onto all the right areas. Apply the highlight using the same technique, always allowing the surface to dry completely between steps. Repeat the highlight step as many times as necessary to achieve the highlight you desire.

One-Stroke Leaves Start the stroke on the chisel edge of the brush, apply pressure and slowly lift the brush, allowing the bristles to return to the chisel edge. This stroke is identical to the comma stroke except it does not have the long tail and it is painted with a flat brush.

Opaque Basecoat Some colors like the reds and oranges are naturally transparent. To basecoat with these colors using the minimum number of layers, mix a little white, tan or cream color into the basecoat color for the fist layer. Example: To basecoat in a bright red, paint the first two layers in red and a touch of white = pink. Then when you add the third layer with the straight red, the red will be clear and bright and cover completely.

S-Stroke Using a flat brush with a sharp chisel edge, start the stroke on the chisel edge. Apply pressure downward, then release and glide back to the chisel edge.

Side-Load Float/Corner Load Use a flat brush in good condition, dampened with water. Touch the corner of the brush into paint, and working in one spot on your waxed palette, firmly brush back and forth to spread the paint evenly across the brush. The brush should have the strong color on one corner and gradually lighten to clean water on the opposite corner. After the brush is properly loaded, use a light touch to apply shading or highlighting.

Soft Floats Moisten the object to be highlighted or shaded with clean water. (I keep a brush and small cup of clean water handy just for this purpose.) No need to stay in any pattern lines. Dampen right over the whole object, not drippy wet, but just enough to make the surface glisten. Using the largest brush suitable for the area, pit-pat on a layer of paint. Deposit the paint slightly away from the edge of the object, then pit-pat it back to the edge of the object. Using this light touch, you can tuck color into corners, soften out colors to get a wide shade or highlight, and achieve a soft, natural look. The premoistened step gives you more time to work before the paint dries, and it diffuses the paint to create a soft look. Let the surface dry completely (if you are in a hurry, keep a hair dryer nearby to speed drying). Repeat the technique one to three times until the desired value of color and width of shaded or highlighted area is achieved.

Spot Shading Use a side-loaded or corner-loaded brush to softly float partially around or under an object. Spot shading is not meant to outline any object, just to accent parts of an object or design.

Stipple Using old brushes or a deerfoot brush, dip the brush into the paint, and punch on your palette or paper towel to blend and remove excess paint. Stipple in an up-and-down motion with a light touch.

Tints A very thin float of an additional color, used to add interest to the design.

Resources

ART CRAFTERS
Bill and Joan Bennett
525 Park Ave.
Lafayette, IN 47904-3256
Tel: (765) 448-1073

HOLLAND BOWL MILL
447 US 131
Sixteenth St.
Box 2102
Holland, MI 49422
Tel: (616) 396-6513

HOLLINS ENTERPRISES,
INC.
670 Orchard Lane
Rt. 35, Box 148
Alpha, OH 45301
Tel: (937) 426-3503
Fax: (937) 426-9726
E-mail: Hollinsent@aol.com

PESKY BEAR
5059 Roszyk Hill Rd.
Machias, NY 14101
Tel/Fax: (716) 942-3250

WAYNE'S WOODENWARE
Wayne and Joan Stabnaw
1913 State Road 150
Neenah, WI 54956-1842
Tel: (920) 725-7986
Fax: (920) 725-9386
For orders only: (800) 840-1497

WOODCRAFTS
Art and Betty Hall
P.O. Box 78
Hwy 67W
Bicknell, IN 47512-0078
Tel: (812) 735-4829
Fax: (812) 735-3187
For orders only: (800) 733-4820

INDEX